Sun Signs
for Lovers

Sun Signs
for Lovers

The astrological guide to love,
sex and relationships

 A GODSFIELD BOOK

Judy Hall

First published in Great Britain in 2005 by
Godsfield Press, a division of
Octopus Publishing Group Ltd
2–4 Heron Quays
Docklands
London E14 4JP

Distributed in the United States and Canada by
Sterling Publishing Co., Inc.
387 Park Avenue South, New York, NY 10016-8810

ISBN 1 84181 246 3
EAN 9781841812465

10 9 8 7 6 5 4 3 2 1

Printed and bound in China

Contents

Introduction

Everyone is interested in love and relationships. If you have picked up this book it will be because you want to understand yourself and your partner or potential lover. You are interested in why you are attracted to some people and turned off by others, why some relationships last days while others are for life. You want to recognize exactly the right partner for you and to avoid the heartbreak that incompatibility can bring. You are interested in whether your sexual style and your expectations and relationship goals are compatible with your current and potential lovers.

The good news is that astrology, through the 12 basic sun signs, can help you to achieve greater harmony in your intimate personal relationships and the great news is that, by taking your understanding of astrology just one simple step further, you can refine the 12 broad basic principles into a unique understanding of yourself, your loved ones and your potential partners. You will learn to recognize and interpret the sexual signals that each sign sends out, as well as understand the confusions that can arise when different parts of the self, as mapped in the birthchart, conflict. Knowing what your partner is really like, or what you yourself truly want, will revolutionize your love life.

This book is a toolkit for good relationships of all kinds. Within these pages you will learn how your sun sign illuminates your personality, relationship style, goals and expectations, sexual fantasies and turn-ons. You will explore how the sun signs of your lovers, partners and friends influence the chemistry of romantic and sexual attraction, and compatibility with partners and personal friends. For example, sun signs can reveal whether people are passionate or romantic, faithful or flirtatious; and whether they are looking for passion or friendship, fidelity or freedom. You will find ways to help an ailing relationship revive, or to pep up an 'all right' one by attuning to your and your partner's secret sexual desires. If you want to move on, it helps to know that signs behave characteristically when breaking up. Foreknowledge can help minimize the trauma of parting, or help find ways for couples to stay together amicably.

Intimacy is about opening and sharing yourself on all levels with someone *other*. It is how close you can allow someone to come to you, and how you can share your thoughts and feelings as well as your lust and your love. To be intimate you need to surrender yourself. You can be truly intimate only if you are completely honest with someone, holding nothing back either out of fear or of favour – which makes you vulnerable, so trust is essential for

intimacy. For some signs this is easy, but for other more suspicious or closed signs, intimacy and trust are an enormous challenge.

Each sun sign shares specific characteristics, although certain traits show up more in one type of relationship than another. If you want to understand how a sign operates, read the whole chapter for the relevant sun sign as this will give you an overview. Then re-read the section relating to your specific relationship.

As you will discover certain signs get on well together; others excite but find it difficult to maintain a relationship for long; other signs actively repel each other. This is because of the subtle shading conveyed to the sun signs by the elements (fire, earth, air and water) and the qualities of cardinal, fixed and mutable (see pages 110 and 122). Understanding the dynamics of the attraction/repulsion cycle around the zodiac wheel can enhance any relationship, and can help you make allowances for a sign's characteristic behaviour, turning a person's actions into 'how they are' rather than 'something they are doing to me'. When you have this understanding, your relationships change dramatically – for the better.

Relationships are complex, multi-layered affairs. There are subtle energies at work and people who, on the surface, should be compatible from a sun sign perspective often turn out not to be so. A special feature of this book is the section devoted to Venus and Mars (see pages 128–141). If your sun sign wasn't spot on, this pair have the answer. They can override the sun sign, or subtly alter or divert its expression.

The powerful desires embodied in Venus send out a siren call to which Mars responds according to its placement in a chart. If Mars is attuned to subtle seduction, the most blatant siren call is ignored. On the other hand, where Mars is in a sign with little subtlety and much passion, sexual fireworks result.

Venus and Mars tell you about your sexuality, which is much more than a question of how often and with whom you have sexual relations. It encompasses your sexual orientation and desires, yes, but it is also how you present yourself, the people you are attracted to and those who repel you. Sexuality pervades every area of your life. Most close interactions have an overt or covert sexual spark to them, whether between same- or opposite-sex lovers, friends or colleagues. You may not do anything about it physically, but the same qualities that attracted you to your lover underlie affinity with your friend or co-worker. And, for some people, friendship is more intimate than sexual relationship.

The sexual zodiac

Aries	♈	Raunchy. Impatient. Too fast? Too bad!
Taurus	♉	Sensual. Savours it slowly. Indefatigable. Can be routine.
Gemini	♊	Sex occurs mostly in the head. Talks continuously.
Cancer	♋	Cuddlesome. Emotional. Won't let go.
Leo	♌	Lustful. Romantic. Larger than life. Exhibitionist.
Virgo	♍	Earthy sensuality. Cool ardour. Has to be perfect.
Libra	♎	Alluring. Amorous. Accommodating. Partner-centred.
Scorpio	♏	Magnetic. Intense. Secretive. Jealous.
Sagittarius	♐	Enthusiastic. Easily bored. The grass is greener elsewhere.
Capricorn	♑	Reserved. Cautious. Surprisingly horny.
Aquarius	♒	Detached. Inventive. Electric. A real one-off!
Pisces	♓	Serial soul mate. In love with love. Swims off but returns.

Part 1

THE SUN SIGNS

The sun represents a particular approach to life which you share with everyone born under your sun sign, but the sun is also your own unique self and the personal qualities you bring to relationship. Characteristics are modified by other factors in your birthchart but, from your sun sign, it is possible to predict how you will behave in love, lust and friendship.

How much of your basic sex drive you express, and how freely you give yourself to others, is shown by the sign under which you were born. Some signs are shy and retiring; others are full-on and unstoppable. Certain sun signs initiate, others react; some live in the inner world of the imagination, others in the external world of action. There are signs that are extrovert exhibitionists, while others take a great deal of coaxing to reveal their carnal desires. Some sun signs love to act out their fantasies, others keep these strictly for their own private viewing.

When you understand your sun sign, you understand your basic sexuality and that of people around you. And when you understand sexuality, you understand all your relationships whether sexually oriented or not.

Aries
the ram

21 March – 19 April
Active • Cardinal • Fire

Passionate and impetuous, Aries is one of the zodiac's raunchiest signs. Lust and libido are strong and energy high, so rapacious Aries has dynamite sex. Your sexual encounters are initiated by you, no matter which sex you are – the lady ram is just as upfront about her sexual needs and lusts as her male counterpart. Impatient and pushy, you make the running and rarely take no for an answer, although if resistance is too strong you quickly lose interest. Tenacity is not your strong point. At the same time you are a romantic at heart. You enjoy the rituals of courtship: the flowers, the presents and the intimate dinners *à deux*, but not the emotional games. When you reach the commitment stage, you may have second thoughts. Independent Aries does not like to be anyone's other half.

What makes you tick: thrusting your way into love

Exuberant Aries is a straightforward soul who has very clear needs and who demands instant gratification. You know what you want, you want it now, and tantrums may ensue if you don't get it. You simply cannot stand frustration, so subtle seduction and playing a waiting game are not for you. You need to be upfront and honest, and you want to be the leader in the relationship.

Partnership is not a state that comes naturally to you and you find it difficult to adjust to other people's needs, especially if these are not immediately apparent. Understanding and empathizing with other people is not one of your strong points as you are 'me'-oriented and very direct, being incapable of hiding your feelings. Transparent yourself, you do not have the guile to manipulate and manoeuvre, and have no patience with people who do.

One of the self-expressive fire signs, you find it easy to impetuously show your emotions, although saying 'I love you' is a little more difficult. You prefer to demonstrate your affection with passionate, and urgent, physicality. But you may be so eager to reach a climax that you forget to listen to what your body is telling you. If you are to find true fulfilment, it would be wise to listen to your own needs – and to those of your partner. Foreplay may be a foreign language to you, but it is one you can learn to advantage.

Aries is a courageous sign and although you can be somewhat self-centred there is a great desire to fight for the underdog and to right wrongs. This brings you into the conflict you thrive on. Your anger is expressed with great heat, but passes just as quickly.

Your style
Active and exciting; pushy, independent, sometimes non-co-operative.

Your relationship style

First impressions are what count with Aries: you are attracted, or you are not. If you are then you see no reason for delay. You express your needs forcefully, and expect your partner, or prospective partner, to respond immediately. Yours can be an insensitive sign and your relationship style is somewhat naive. Finding it hard to distinguish between love and desire, you fall head over heals in lust, and sometimes into marriage as well. But the desire can pass just as quickly.

Your seduction technique

Intensely passionate, your seduction style is brash, blatant and totally honest. You want to conquer and get it on without delay. Neither sex waits to be asked nor can you stand frustration. Sexually provocative and pushy, you are impatient for sex, and you always take the lead. A prospective partner may find him- or herself having sex in the most unlikely places.

You say
'Me first!'

What you seek
Short, sharp sex; love, lifelong lust, romance and adventure, faithfulness, challenge and a degree of commitment.

What turns you on

With your fiery, passionate nature life is a turn-on and it takes little to set your libido in motion. A smouldering look is enough; your imagination does the rest. The surface of your head is an erogenous zone, especially your hair and your lips, and Aries enjoys kisses that devour, but if your partner wants to inflame you, stroking the nape of your neck starts a conflagration.

You and your fantasy

Aries fantasy is hot, fast and furious, but curiously romantic. It is also very active, both sexes are the knight on a white charger rushing in to rescue the damsel, or dude, in distress – you relish risk. Many of your fantasies involves its modern-day equivalent, a superstud riding a mean machine, but you also enjoy an encounter with a scarlet woman. Dressing up excites you. Occasionally you prefer to watch and may orchestrate a three-in-a-bed scene.

How you behave as a partner

As a partner there are times when you behave romantically, showering your partner with gifts and, occasionally, expressing your feelings with flowery sentiment; but equally you can behave with great selfishness, or are utterly insensitive and inconsiderate. Aries finds the whole notion of equal partnership problematic, preferring to dominate the situation, and can take time to adjust to being part of a pair. You function best as your independent self and there are times when you simply go ahead and do what you sincerely think is right without consulting your partner, which can lead to friction. This is not done with the intention of upsetting your partner, it is simply you being you and a partner who understands this has a much better chance of retaining your devotion.

Trust and intimacy
Finds it challenging.

Secret sexual desire
Sex with a stranger.

As a fire sign you love to flirt and wise partners give you plenty of leeway in this respect recognizing that you will probably go home with the person you arrived with.

You are seeking a soul mate, a life-partner, and if someone comes close to your ideal, or appears to, your impetuosity can rush you into matrimony. Once there the flaws may rapidly become apparent but you continue to hope, although yours is not the most faithful sign in the world. Even if you are in a long-term relationship, your need for fast sex and constant stimulation may lead to brief affairs. You do not feel disloyal to your partner when you indulge in a one-night stand but you may not be so forgiving if your partner strays. While not jealous, you are hot-blooded and your need to come first with your partner can be offended by someone who shares amorous glances with another.

What you expect from a partner

Unswerving loyalty and total attention from your partner is demanded as a right; you simply cannot conceive of your partner having time for anyone else or having a life outside the relationship. Your partner could well believe that you have this image of a box in which your partner lives until you are ready to take them out to play or mate.

When it ends

A relationship is likely to end with you storming out. You may not intend to stay out – like your ardour your anger is easily aroused but cools just as quickly – but your partner may have other views. Rather than saying 'sorry' you have sex to make up. However, once you have finally parted, you put it behind you and get on with life as quickly as possible.

Aries relationships

Understanding your Aries man

Aries is the original macho man of the zodiac; he is the most immediate and primal expression of masculinity. He just loves to feel he is protecting his woman – and Aries always wants to be on top. Going all out for what he wants, Aries man is active and volatile, as easily roused to anger as to passion. There is nothing cool or laid-back about this lusty male. Aries wants to dominate and make his mark on the world: fast. Do not expect him to show patience or to understand nuances and subtleties. He acts on his instincts, spontaneously without pause for thought, and is intensely involved in the business of living. Leading from way out front, he craves adventure and learns through his experiences.

What you need to understand about your Aries man is that he is convinced he is right. He knows everything there is to know, and woe betide you if you try to give him directions or put him straight. Highly competitive, he hates to make a mistake or to be seen to fail. No matter how tempting, never remind him of occasions when he did just that. Praise him, flatter him and work your way around the danger zone, then quietly put things right. There are times when he tests your tolerance, and your ability to forgive, to the limits.

Aries man

Passion rating
★★★★★

How to make it work
Let him make the running, be lavish in your praise, surprise him, and act defenceless even if you're not.

Understanding your Aries woman

Like her male counterpart, Aries woman is active, spontaneous and macho. Caring nothing for feminine wiles, she gets her way through direct confrontation and inspired leadership. This is a dominant woman who knows what she wants and goes all out to get it, and yet has a charming quality of naive innocence about her. Pushy as she might be, it is impossible to be angry with this bodacious companion for long. Just because she is macho, however, does not mean that she is unfeminine. She likes to be wooed and relishes romantic gestures such as the presentation of a single red rose.

If you let her take the lead, she rewards you with undying devotion. Try to take charge and she dumps you in disgust.

Aries woman

Passion rating
★ ★ ★ ★ ★

How to make it work
Let her be the boss, surprise her with flowers and wild sex as you walk through the door.

Other relationships

Aries is an extremely straightforward sign: what you see is what you get – which means that your Aries friend is honest, faithful and opinionated. An adrenaline junkie, he, or she, expects you to keep up with a multitude of activities, many of them sports based and almost all carrying danger to life and limb. You have an active social life together; there are plenty of opportunities to make new friends and to try out new adventures. If your Aries friend is female, you'll be invited to try all the latest health kicks and no one is more supportive when you start a diet – or quicker to urge you to let it go.

Like all rams Aries wants to be leader of the pack and you need to be tactful if you intend to introduce new ideas or a different way of doing things. Fortunately this spontaneous sign is fairly flexible; as long as you do not dominate the scene, your Aries friend goes along with your suggestions – for a time. Then they are adopted as Aries' own, or flamboyantly dropped for something more stimulating.

Aries has a fiery temper and a low boredom threshold, and many argue for the sake of arguing. They get off on challenge and conflict. If you value peace and quiet do not be provoked, but if you too enjoy a challenge, debate and argue with vigour and you'll make your Aries friend a happy ram. This sign never bears a grudge and asserts the right of everyone to their own opinion, so there is no comeback if you disagree.

In times of crisis you can call on Aries to help you fight battles and right wrongs, but not to give you emotional support. This sign doesn't understand emotions and finds secrets tiresome and impossible to keep.

Aries is not a team player; this is the most independent sign in the zodiac so it can be difficult for Aries to be a co-worker. Aries does not know how to co-operate, and rarely has time to learn; Aries wants to lead from out front, and is brilliant at initiating. What Aries finds exceedingly tedious is carrying things through to their conclusion. With Aries for a co-worker you find yourself picking up the pieces and carrying on regardless, as Aries rarely stops to delegate or to explain. But there are advantages: things have a habit of happening around Aries. This is where the action is – and promotion too because generous Aries gives credit where credit is due and you get to share in the glory. On the other hand you may find yourself carrying the can when things go wrong. Aries is not averse to slipping out of difficult situations and rarely stays around to take the blame!

Compatibility chart

Aries ★ ★ ★	Libra ★ ★ ★ ★ ★
Taurus ★	Scorpio ★ ★ ★
Gemini ★ ★ ★ ★	Sagittarius ★ ★ ★ ★ ★
Cancer ★ ★	Capricorn ★ ★ ★
Leo ★ ★ ★ ★ ★	Aquarius ★ ★
Virgo ★ ★ ★	Pisces ★

Taurus

the bull

20 April – 21 May
Passive • Fixed • Earth

Taurus is the most sensual sign of the zodiac. Your indolent appearance gives little indication of your passionate nature and strong libido – until you are aroused by carnal desire, when seductiveness oozes out of every pore. Seeking a love object, you prefer to attract slowly, savouring the moment, and are tenacious in your approach. Beauty is a great turn-on for you. Luxury-loving and pleasure-oriented, you indulge every sense, especially that of taste. Taurus loves good food, and eating is an essential part of your sexual ritual. Your life is not ruled by lust – with your cautious nature and strong control over your instincts you are too concerned with your own security to jeopardize it by acting precipitately. When you are sure, your partner becomes the centre of your world and you are jealous and possessive. You want a relationship that lasts for life.

What makes you tick: sensing your way into love

Security is your biggest concern. You want your life to be safe, orderly and predictable, and you expect promises to be kept. You abhor change and need time to adjust, even when it involves something as exciting as a new lover. Treading cautiously, you make very certain before committing yourself but once you fall in love, it tends to be forever. Although Taurus is a receptive sign, emotional introspection does not come easily to you and you find it extremely difficult to discuss your feelings.

While you are turned on by physical attractiveness, more mundane concerns lie behind your choice of mate. You want to be sure you can enjoy a comfortable lifestyle. Comfort and the material trappings of a relationship – the house, the car, the married state – mean a great deal to you. Once you have these, you are loathe to let them go and remain in a relationship long after it has become stultified 'because of the house'. One of the most important things for your partner to learn is how to coax gently you into something new. The slightest sign of coercion and you refuse to budge.

Your style

Exceedingly loyal and immovable; reliable, tenacious and utterly trustworthy.

Your relationship style

You move in slowly, building up gradually and savouring each moment until you reach the forceful climax. Averse to risk, you want your sex to be safe and predictable but thoroughly enjoyable. Taurus takes relationships seriously and you prefer one partner to whom you are committed for life. To show your love you take your partner out on the town, and give intimate dinners for close friends. Your generous nature enjoys giving and receiving tangible love tokens and you display physical affection, touch being an important part of a relationship for you.

Your seduction technique

'Out on the pull' exactly describes how you operate. You carefully size up all possibilities and never attract someone just because you feel randy. Only if there is someone who pleases your eye do you turn on your irresistible magnets. When aroused you exude sexuality and your intent to seduce is signalled well ahead of time.

What turns you on

The senses are the erogenous zone for Taurus. You enjoy deep, tonguing kisses and your taste buds are a source of great titillation; being fed tasty titbits spurs you on. Sensual perfume and the feel of silk on your skin sets your body afire as does stroking, kneading and sucking round your neck.

You and your fantasy

Your fantasies involve luxurious surroundings, exotic food, sensual pleasure and total pampering, with a harem of willing partners. More than a few orgies take place in your head. Whether this is

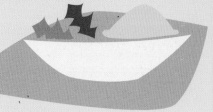

translated into action is debatable but sex-play with delicacies such as whipped cream or chocolate is likely. The darker side of your fantasies around pleasure and pain remain strictly within the privacy of your own mind.

How you behave as a partner

Taurus is partnership-oriented but you sometimes see your partner as an extension of yourself, or as a status symbol. You may take your partner for granted, not being neglectful but rather overlooking the small courtesies of loving attention. You tend to have strictly allocated nights for sex and anything different throws you out of your routine.

You rarely feel the need to work on your relationship, and you may be unaware that your partner is bored and in need of something new. Because you are loyal and faithful, you take it for granted that your partner is too. In your eyes your partner's place is by your side and you do not stand by placidly while flirting occurs, no matter how light-hearted this may be. You are a possessive soul and woe betide anyone who moves in to pay attention to your partner – or the partner whose amorous glance alights elsewhere. Taurus has a terrible temper, rarely shown, which may explode when fuelled by your legendary jealousy. Any indiscretion is held against your partner for the life of the relationship and brooded on resentfully; forgiveness is not your strong suit.

Deeply in touch with your body and sense-oriented, there is a danger that physical sensation is everything to you. Subtle emotion is not your forte but sharing your feelings with your partner deepens your connection and helps you to communicate at an emotional level.

What you expect from a partner

Absolute integrity and faithfulness are essential to you. You must be able to trust your partner utterly and to know that his or her primary loyalty is to you. You expect your partner to support you and to provide a good home and the financial and emotional security you seek. You also expect your partner to be willing and sense-orientated in meeting your sexual and social desires.

When it ends

Endings are terribly difficult for Taurus and you do everything in your power to keep a relationship going no matter how dead it has become. The appearance of a stable partnership and the trappings of success are more important than the actuality and, for you, separation equates to being torn out by your roots. Always resistant to change, you dislike intensely the thought of divorce, not the least because it means dividing up the spoils (your possessiveness extends to material goods). You particularly want to keep the house and the car. Your partner will find you obstructive and obstinate and you hold on long after a divorce has gone through.

Trust and intimacy

Slow to trust, resistant to intimacy.

Secret sexual desire

Body piercing.

Taurus relationships

Understanding your Taurus man

Earthy and practical, this man belongs to one of the most sensual and tenacious signs of the zodiac. Although an excellent lover, he is somewhat lacking in imagination but compensates with a powerful libido and enormous staying power. He thrives on indolent sensual experiences, both sexual and material. Once he is committed to you, he gives you his all, and expects the same in return. This is one of the most jealous and possessive signs of the zodiac, and a Taurus never forgets – forgiveness is enormously difficult for him.

Taurus man

Passion rating
★ ★ ★ ★

How to make it work
Proceed slowly, introduce change very, very gradually; and remain faithful.

To understand your Taurus man, you need to know that everything he does is oriented towards his security: he needs to feel stable, safe and comfortable. If pushed outside his comfort zone, he becomes stubborn and dogmatic. Faced with inevitable change he tries to hold it back no matter what the cost to himself or others.

While your Taurus man is superb in a practical crisis, he is hopeless in an emotional one. He dislikes dramas or tantrums and simply withdraws his attention. Wise partners reserve such displays of emotion for friends who can cope. In most matters, however, your Taurus man is supportive, although he can be downright bossy as he believes his advice is the best.

Do not rush your Taurus man. He likes to do things deliberately and to follow his tried and tested routine. When leaving the house he has to gather everything up, check, and then check again. He cannot hurry, nor will he be hurried. If you push he becomes an immovable object, which is bad news if you happen to be in bed at the time! Nothing stops Taurus libido quite as dead in its tracks as a sudden move or an improper suggestion – the impropriety being timing rather than content. This is a man who cannot do two things at once, especially when it comes to thinking and moving. It also helps you to know that, while a generous soul at heart, Taurus likes to look after the money. He spends lavishly on luxury and opulence, but he'd prefer it if you asked first so that he can check for quality and good workmanship. This is a man who has strong values and knows his own mind.

Understanding your Taurus woman

Your Taurus woman is a complex mix of sensuality and practicality. Her luscious body has underclothes of silk, and a thick woollen jumper over the top to keep her warm. Valuing comfort even more than her male counterpart, she craves certainty and security. A woman of great appetites, she needs plenty of earthy sex to keep her satisfied and sensible partners buy stocks of delicious food to keep up her stamina. In return she gives you loyalty and faithfulness, and a thoroughly erotic time.

Your Taurus woman appreciates quality; whether in or out of bed, she demands the best. If you want to keep her happy, supply her with sumptuous gifts in the finest materials. The gift can be as practical as you like: this delights her Taurus heart, as long as it is expensive.

Taurus woman

Passion rating
★ ★ ★ ★

How to make it work
Pamper her, remain faithful; never hurry her or give her a cheap present.

Other relationships

Taurus is a faithful and reliable lifelong friend who needs a fixed routine rather than surprises: allow at least three days' notice of a prospective outing, and preferably a month. Given that, Taurus is excellent company especially for artistic or foodie pursuits.

Your Taurus friend wants to be involved in your life; decision-making and planning come naturally to this pragmatic sign who is full of good advice – and who can be exceedingly bossy if you don't take that advice. Do not consult your Taurus friend if you are planning life changes: Taurus hates those, but your friend can certainly help you out in practical ways. This sign excels at do-it-yourself, gardening and car maintenance. If your crisis is to do with relationships, bear in mind that

Taurus goes for the 'stay at all costs' option and does not understand emotions. Nor is Taurus good at lending you money if your crisis is financial, even where this is temporary. In his or her eyes you should have made provision well in advance.

Don't under any circumstances expect your Taurus friend to rough it. This is a sign that values comfort highly and a Taurean has a certain standard below which he or she will not go, especially where food is concerned. Avoid the fast-food outlet and head for a decent restaurant if you want to keep your friend sweet-tempered.

Finally, bear in mind that Taurus is an exceedingly possessive sign and your Taurus friend, while gregarious and sociable, does not like to share you. You may need tactfully to extricate yourself from arrangements that bind you too tightly to this tenacious sign.

Taurus is an extremely conscientious and highly reliable sign, and the most hard-working. Long after everyone else has packed up and gone home, Taurus is beavering away to finish what is needed for the morning – or the week after next. So, if there are vital jobs to do, give them to dependable Taurus. Don't forget to thank your Taurus co-worker appropriately, though; they are so often taken for granted.

If you're having a party, ask your Taurus co-worker along; this indulgent sign is into pleasure so make sure the food is gourmet standard. But the invitation would be wise because Taurus hates to be left out. It is important never to upset your Taurus co-worker: remember his or her birthday, do whatever you promise and never let them down.

Compatibility chart

Aries ★	Libra ★ ★
Taurus ★ ★ ★ ★ ★	Scorpio ★ ★ ★ ★ ★
Gemini ★ ★ ★	Sagittarius ★ ★
Cancer ★	Capricorn ★ ★ ★ ★ ★
Leo ★ ★ ★	Aquarius ★ ★ ★
Virgo ★ ★ ★ ★ ★	Pisces ★ ★ ★ ★

Gemini

the twins

22 May – 20 June
Active • Mutable • Air

Gemini is the most communicative, flirtatious, inventive and persuasive sign in the zodiac: pillow talk, phone sex and internet chat rooms suit Gemini. But, while delighting in the idea of love, you are not into lifelong involvement. Other people are important as a foil for your thoughts rather than as a vehicle for your lust. You enjoy discussing feelings, preferably someone else's rather than your own, but have no desire to immerse yourself in emotion. A quick fling is fine, but Gemini may spend more time fantasizing about sex than actually participating. Not that anyone would know that to listen to you: according to you you are having the most wonderful sex life ever. Gemini can convince anyone of anything, and less eloquent signs find themselves finessed into bed without really knowing how they got there!

What makes you tick: talking your way into love

You need other people to make you spark. Delighting in word games, you come alive when you can share your ideas and satisfy your insatiable curiosity, and, of course, when communicating with the world. As a dual sign, two-faced and multifaceted, you flit seamlessly from one thing to another, without even noticing that you have changed your views or your personality. Other signs find it hard to keep up, and also to understand that, for you, truth is whatever you happen to be embracing momentarily. It can easily change, and you play devil's advocate to keep things interesting. So, when you vow eternal love, it is neither truth nor lie: it is what it is *at that moment*. It might perhaps be better for you to put a proviso on it, but how can you when you yourself don't know when it will change? A partner needs to know that you are not deliberately trying to deceive – half the time you don't know how you feel and so you are fooling yourself as well.

Your partner also needs to know that you hate to be bored, that you become mischievous, and at times positively lethal, if your mind is not well occupied. Gazing into someone's eyes for hours on end is your idea of hell! And Gemini should never be asked to keep a secret; it is an impossibility! You were born to gossip.

Your style
Bright, gossipy, inventive, intellectual, fickle.

Your relationship style
You find it difficult to be restricted to only one partner and often marry late, particularly as you enjoy platonic friendships with both sexes. There is a sexual frisson to those friendships that just might develop further. For you, mental rapport is much more important than physical considerations and you want your partner to be a companion in all

senses of the word. Even when you succumb to love, commitment is a problem, as is faithfulness, but your versatility finds an outlet in working through the Kama Sutra. The difficulty is that relationships happen in your head and you may be so caught up in the excitement of your erotic fantasies that you forget about real relationships.

Your seduction technique

Gemini is a cool sign but you enjoy the hearts and flowers approach to romance, and you rise to the challenge of bewitching a prospective partner into bed. Your silver-tongued subtle seduction may promise a lasting relationship but this is not the truth, especially as you enjoy flirting and clever verbal foreplay, which is intended to amuse rather than lead to other things.

What turns you on

Aural sex is what gets you going, your erogenous zone is between your ears but it may become oral. Talking, thinking and fantasizing about sex turns you on and whispered sweet nothings or talking dirty is highly erotic, as is a tongue exploring your ear. Such delights can occur entirely in your imagination, or with a phone or a computer as a partner. While heavy touch is a turn-off, light stroking of your palm and nibbling your fingers and toes works wonders for you, as does reading erotica or watching soft porn.

You and your fantasy

Your fantasies roam far and wide, you never run out of ideas, and anything can happen in your fertile imagination. Virtual sex is ideal for you as there is excitement without emotional content. With your low boredom threshold, fantasies have to be quick-fire and ever-changing. You may fantasize about red-hot, carnal passion or orgies. Occasionally, out of curiosity, you try these and may use porn as a quick turn-on.

How you behave as a partner

Your partner is unlikely to receive unadulterated attention, even in the first flush of love. You are into crowds rather than twosomes. There is always someone else you want to talk to, or flirt with.

You are less likely to stray if you are given space but, as you find it hard to commit and as you get bored easily, love affairs just seem to happen. A flirt rather than a philanderer, you didn't mean to end up in bed, it didn't mean anything to you – but your partner sees things differently. Your partner is aware of all those phone calls you hide, the internet messages you hastily erase, the friends at work that you pop out for a drink with. You may think you are being sociable, your partner knows otherwise.

Trust and intimacy
Superficial, verbal.

Secret sexual desire
Being ravished.

As a partner one of your greatest failings is that you do not really listen, especially if your partner is saying something deeply emotional, or touches on sore points in your relationship. You are not given to emotional intimacy. It is not a question of not trusting someone else – you trust everyone – more that you don't know your true feelings yourself so sharing them with a partner is impossible. If your partner shares intimate secrets, he or she may be devastated to find that you discuss them with all and sundry. There is nothing Gemini likes more than a good gossip and you are unlikely to consider your partner's feelings in the matter.

What you expect from a partner

You want a flexible partner who is sociable and outgoing, who enjoys partying and gossiping, and who is not dependent on you for company. You expect your partner to give you the space to pursue your other interests. Above all, you expect your partner to be entertaining and well-informed. You value intellectual companionship and you need to be able to discuss a myriad subjects together and, while you enjoy explaining things, stupidity or slow thinking bores the pants off you. Good looks are nowhere near as important to you as a good mind.

When it ends

Gemini is a master of the fast exit. For you it is off with the old and on with the new. Lightly committed and with so many other things to occupy your mind, you could well overlook your partner's absence. Quickie divorce was invented for Gemini because, by the time it comes around, you are ensconced with your next partner and happy to give your ex the world.

Gemini relationships

Understanding your Gemini man

You never really know your Gemini man, he'll always surprise you. A superficial and yet incredibly complex, multi-layered character, although he has intellectual depths, he doesn't know how to make an emotional connection or how to be intimate at that deep level where emotional sharing takes place. Instead he dances lightly over the surface of life.

It is not so much understand your man as understand your men. Mercurial Gemini changes his disposition in a moment, switching before your ears. He is winsome, witty, satirical, sarcastic, informative, derogatory and defamatory. He holds one opinion, then argues the opposite, and swings back again. You need to be agile to keep up. This man can be quickly overtaken by black moods when, for once, he insists on being alone. Just when you begin to despair, his mood inexplicably lightens.

This sociable character has an insatiable need for people. Wired, he bounces around a gathering mixing, fixing and getting it on. He has several mobile phones because he cannot stand call waiting. He simply has to talk, even in his sleep. And he cannot resist the lure of an enticing woman, or a good debate. This sign never grows old, his face remains unlined, his chat-up lines still work, and he is charming and mentally active to the end.

Gemini man

Passion rating
★★

How to make it work
Be interesting, know a little about everything, and prepare to improvise.

Gemini is naturally irresponsible: this elusive man never faces the consequences of his actions. Somehow he leads a charmed life, the gods love his untruths and his dissemblings. They smile on his schemes and honey his words. Concepts such as eternity, dependability and commitment, while intellectually diverting for him, have no real meaning. But amusing, intriguing and bemusing, this man is an engaging companion who knows how to have fun.

Understanding your Gemini woman

A Gemini woman is even more mercurial than her male counterpart. She can be slinky and seductive or, in a flash, cool and aloof. She gets into toy boys not because she thinks they make her look good, but rather because, mentally, she has not aged. She revels in youth, beauty, wit and playfulness. More interested in relationships than a male Gemini, her sexual inventiveness astounds you; but don't be fooled, this lady has great difficulty with commitment and emotional intimacy. She finds other people's feelings fascinating, but is totally out of touch with her own. A word of warning: don't trust her with your secrets, gossip is her life blood.

Gemini woman

Passion rating
★★✦

How to make it work
Remember that she needs to talk, flirt and gossip. If you don't provide an entertaining sounding board, someone else will.

Other relationships

Gemini makes a wonderful friend if you want a sociable, fun companion to party with; if you enjoy long, gossipy chats over coffee; or if you want to sit up with a bottle of wine putting the world to rights long into the night. But if you want a friend for deep, intimate conversations, someone who cherishes your secrets, look elsewhere. Your Gemini friend relishes the chats, but your secrets are all over town by morning.

Where a Gemini friend comes into their own is when you need advice. Gemini is the natural fixer, always knowing the answer, or precisely where to go for what you need. The advice you get from this friend is practical and to the point – unless it's about emotions, in which case it is only theory. This is the friend who talks about anything and everything, so this is your chance to shed your inhibitions and open up. It is unlikely that you will shock your Gemini friend who comes up with exciting ideas to spice up your love life. (Keep a notebook handy and you could have a best-selling book of erotica by the end of the evening.)

Gregarious Gemini doesn't go in for singularity or depth, and this sign tends to have lots of acquaintances rather than one 'best friend'. You'll be one of a crowd and you may not always hold your friend's attention but you will have a great time, and you'll learn a lot!

At work Gemini is at his or her best in an environment where communication is vital. Bright and bubbly to have around, Gemini is dedicated to passing on facts and figures. Most of the information he or she gives will be accurate, but it is worth checking as Gemini can be slapdash, especially if the contents are dull. Your Gemini co-worker rarely stops to listen to instructions.

This is the co-worker who chats and gossips, and gossips and chats. They have all the juicy titbits and you hear it first from a Gemini. Prone to talking about other people behind their back but sometimes just in earshot, with Gemini's flair for sliding out of trouble it looks as though you were the one who was gossiping. Make it clear from the outset that you are not interested in character assassination. But if you do you'll miss out on being included in your Gemini co-workers active social life.

Compatibility chart

Aries ★★★ Libra ★★★★

Taurus ★ Scorpio ★

Gemini ★★★★★ Sagittarius ★★★★★

Cancer ★ Capricorn ★★

Leo ★★★ Aquarius ★★★★

Virgo ★★★★ Pisces ★

Cancer

the crab

21 June – 22 July
Passive • Cardinal • Water

Tender-hearted Cancer is one of the most caring and emotionally sensitive signs, needing to be needed and to belong. For you love is an emotional melding; you seek closeness in an intimacy beyond words and yet can shut yourself off. Hiding your passionate nature under a shell of cool containment, in the safety of your home a sexy siren is revealed. Flowing with the currents of your emotional nature, passion rises and falls and security needs direct much of your behaviour. You enjoy sexual relations within a loving marriage, and home and family are important. Cuddles are as vital as sex, and you seek your partner's unadulterated love. Your weak spots are possessiveness and jealousy. Once your crab's claws take hold, they rarely let go and there is a ruthless streak hidden deep inside your soft interior.

What makes you tick: obliquely feeling your way into love

Cancer is a deeply private sign and you need to feel very safe indeed before you reveal yourself. Despite being tough and confident on the outside, your inner world is insecure and you seek constant reassurance that you are loved and needed. A partner has to be overly demonstrative to satisfy this. You want to protect those you love: for you your partner is your child and you can have a tendency to smother-love.

With your powerful urge towards home-making, your way of showing love is with food and if your partner rejects your food, you yourself feel rejected. Cancer is touchy and sensitive to the slightest rebuff; or what you perceive as rebuff, you take things personally.

Everything you do is oblique, and oriented towards security. Home means a great deal to both sexes. You want to get to the top so you can love and protect your partner in the best way you know, by being safe financially. Feeling poor unless you have thousands in the bank, you have a nest egg put by 'just in case'. You fear poverty because it makes you feel vulnerable, and you do not appreciate anyone spending your money. There can be a mean streak in Cancer, born out of that fear and your natural caution, and you worry that you have been taken advantage of even when you have found a bargain.

Despite your desire for physical closeness, you also have a cyclical need to withdraw and process your emotions. Your emotional tides are ruled by the moon. At the dark of the moon, you are at your most moody and vulnerable and your partner may feel shut out.

Your style
Caring but possessive; quietly nurturing and supportive.

Your relationship style

Eternally romantic, once you have committed yourself to a partner, you are faithful and loyal. There are times when your partner feels smothered by your love. Fiercely possessive, you demand constant displays of affection and woe betide the partner who forgets an anniversary.

Sentimental occasions mean a great deal to you and, when courting, you put on the full works: a romantic candlelit dinner, expensive presents and a great time in bed afterwards. When you get married you want to involve the whole family.

Your seduction technique

Once you set your sights on someone you seldom let go. With your clinging nature, your seduction technique is security-oriented and you are more likely to seduce someone you know. You want a long-term partner whom you can rely on and to whom you can open up your inner self. For this reason you reject one-night stands in favour of commitment.

What turns you on

The breasts are the major erogenous zone for Cancer. Stroking, squeezing and sucking the nipples is a great turn-on, although Cancer is almost as aroused by cuddling. You need to know you are wanted. The stomach is another erotic zone, especially if loving is accompanied by a sensual feast. Cancer invented edible body paint but may prefer strawberries and cream, or a fruit-scented bath.

You and your fantasy

Cancer's fantasies are imaginative, romantic and private. They often include water and usually involve a handsome prince or princess who seduces you with the promise of 'happily ever after'. In the privacy of your own head, you allow yourself to take risks that you would never pursue in reality. You need to trust your partner utterly before you reveal your fantasies, and even then you hesitate to act them out.

How you behave as a partner

As soon as you have made up your mind that this is 'the one', you want to formalize the arrangement. Unlikely to live with anyone when you can marry, you want the knot tied, the papers signed and the house purchased. Then you set about making a home.

Cancer is extremely sentimental. You remember the day you met, when you first kissed, the first time you went to bed together, as well as when you got engaged, married and had a child; and you want to celebrate all these important occasions, preferably with the whole family present.

A tactile sign you express your love physically, and seek reassurance, so you want to hold hands and sit and cuddle for hours. However, this is not only because you need to demonstrate your closeness. Physical contact acts as a 'keep off' sign to other people. You are possessive about your partner and do not tolerate any hint of infidelity. Even if the relationship is dying on its feet, you will do all you can to hold on. Your partner finds him- or herself coddled, nurtured and spoiled.

Both sexes tend to mother their partner and to project unfinished business from childhood into the relationship, seeking what you failed to find in your own parents. As a result your partner pulls back. Highly emotional yourself, you so easily feel rejected by your partner and constantly seek to re-tie the knot.

Trust and intimacy

Cautious trust, superficial intimacy.

Secret sexual desire

Starring in a porn movie.

What you expect from a partner

Loyalty and faithfulness, together with a full-time, full-on relationship, is what you demand from your partner. It is as though you are emotionally joined at the hip. You expect to be the whole of his or her life, with no room for outside interests, and you demand children and a settled home as tangible symbols of commitment.

When it ends

This is when the real meaning of those clinging crab's claws becomes obvious, and where you discover emotional hell. You want to stay in the house and hold on to all your possessions, especially children. Your ruthless streak emerges, no way are you giving anything up. You make divorce as difficult as possible, and try to seduce your partner back even if you were the one to leave.

Cancer relationships

Understanding your Cancer man

Understanding this complex and highly sensitive man is quite a task. At first he shows a tough, invulnerable outer shell but as you get to know him better, and particularly once you have experienced the great tides of emotion that sweep through him, you realize that underneath there is a vulnerable and soft-hearted man who is deeply affected by his feelings. You perceive his neediness and the pain he feels for the suffering of others. But then, just when you think you have sussed him out, he shows his tough, not to say ruthless, side.

This man has a shrewd mind and is highly ambitious: he wants to get to the top and he would like your support. But, oblique as always, he is unlikely to ask directly. He can easily fall into an attack of 'poor me', or into brooding moodiness. A wise partner looks at the moon before wondering what is up. This man is attuned to the moon, particularly at the new and full phases. Encourage him to take time for himself at the dark of the moon and he will be more stable and far less moody. If the moon is not the cause, check whether he is sulking because of something you said. He senses a slight in the most innocent of remarks; not that he'll tell you, you'll have to coax it out of him – and make a grovelling apology before he is happy again.

Cancer man

Passion rating
★ ★ ★ ★

How to make it work
Feed, nurture and care for your Cancer man and share your feelings with him. Let him protect you, he needs to be needed.

Understanding your Cancer woman

A Cancer woman shows her emotions to a greater extent than a Cancer man, and is even more sensitive and prone to mood swings because her menstrual cycle is ruled by the moon. Cosseting and reassuring her with physical contact is more effective than asking what is wrong.

Focused closely on home and family, and at times having her identity reflected back through a successful husband, this woman nonetheless has powerful, if well-camouflaged, ambitions and may wish to combine a career with being the perfect wife and mother. She juggles these successfully provided the home is stable and you give her every support, but you could easily find yourself being treated like one of the children and your sex life could suffer as her libido is the first thing to go.

Other relationships

If you want a kind, caring, considerate and endlessly thoughtful friend, look no further than Cancer. This is someone who longs for a 'best friend' to share everything with. But if you value your personal liberty, you may want to think twice. This sign needs to be needed and this is a person with a strong nesting instinct. She, or he, is in and out of your home constantly, arriving with sustenance 'just in case'. Your Cancer friend finds it hard to understand personal space, and feels deeply slighted if you suggest you need it.

Notwithstanding this is a great friend to have if you want a shoulder to cry on, or need a someone with whom to watch a sloppy, sentimental movie. Cancer loves emotion and emoting, and gives an excellent back rub. Get out the old photos, sigh over past lovers, tell the story of your life, and your Cancer friend is happy to listen, as long as you do the same. Indeed it won't be long before your Cancer friend starts telling you how much worse off he, or she, is. This sign has a huge capacity for self-pity, and for manipulation. Watch out for those crocodile tears or the story that tugs at your heartstrings. Cancer is a past master at getting his or her own way.

You will soon be aware how moody and manipulative this sign can be. It is always worth checking you haven't inadvertently done something to upset your friend, which is easy to do, but it is often more a question of hormones, moon cycles and over-sensitivity. But, if you can cope with these, you have a friend for life whose shrewd advice can be extremely helpful.

Cancer co-workers are the social workers of the zodiac. Nurturing and caring, Cancer is the person who makes the coffee, brings cake, has the flu remedies waiting, and gets the birthday cards signed – in between sorting out any little problems that arise and doing the work of anyone who is off sick. Cancer can't help it: the urge to mother is strong, even in Cancer men.

And yet your Cancer co-worker hides an ambitious streak that means that one day your co-worker may be your boss. You won't know that he or she applied for the job – Cancer is not going to be upfront about it. You might have applied for the job yourself, but shrewd Cancer sidles in and takes it from under your nose. When that happens Cancer will settle old scores, so make sure you do not inadvertently slight your sensitive Cancer co-worker, or fail to appreciate all those little kindnesses now. Tomorrow could be too late.

Compatibility chart

Aries ★★★   Libra ★★★★

Taurus ★★   Scorpio ★★★★★

Gemini ★   Sagittarius ★

Cancer ★★★★★   Capricorn ★★★

Leo ★   Aquarius ★★★

Virgo ★★★   Pisces ★★★★★

Leo
the lion

23 July – 22 August
Active • Fixed • Fire

Love makes the world go round for Leo. Yours is a fiery, passionate sign and you dislike being alone. Romance is an essential ingredient for Leo's happiness. You thoroughly enjoy the whole process of dating – the flowers, the presents, the wining and dining – and this doesn't stop when wedding bells have rung. Anniversaries will be marked by larger-than-life gestures such as a box at the opera or the best hotel suite in town. You like to see and be seen and want to show off all your assets, including your partner. With your gregarious nature and sexual magnetism, you spend a great deal of time holding court, but not so much so that there is no time for sexual athleticism. As a hot-blooded lion, you take every opportunity to satisfy your powerful sex drive. The love life of a flamboyant Leo is never dull.

What makes you tick: opening your heart to love

Leo is happiest in a warm, loving, sexually active relationship with a partner, or out hunting with the pack. As a fixed fire sign, you need excitement but look for security and certainty. You are quite capable of making things dramatic by your own actions, craving admiration and adulation. You want your partner to look up to you and are, dare we mention the word, bossy: autocratic Leo likes to be in control.

Appearances are extremely important to you and you hate to be seen at less than your dignified best. You are proud when the special someone you are with looks good because you feel this reflects well on you.

As a Leo you are king, or queen, of the zodiac and feel that your rightful place is somewhat elevated above lesser mortals. Fortunately your good-natured charm and sunny disposition ensure that lesser mortals do not find this offensive. Indeed most Leos are besieged by willing subjects satisfying your need to be adored. If you can't find someone to love you, you settle for lust or, failing that, for admiration.

A creature of habit, you may stay with a partner because, in your eyes, any lover – provided he or she is presentable – is better than none. This highlights what you would prefer to keep hidden: beneath that sunny face and ebullient manner, Leo often lacks confidence.

Your style

Co-operative, but Leo wants to be in charge; gregarious but loyal.

Your relationship style

A romantic at heart with a generous nature, you shower your lover with gifts and flamboyant gestures. In return you expect fidelity, protestations of undying love and total loyalty. You need intimacy and sexual closeness but can be naively trusting, taking people at face value unless they show themselves to be something other. Your vanity will not allow you to chase after someone who does not show immediate interest, nor does your pride reveal a broken heart. No matter how hurt you are, you put on a brave smile.

Your seduction technique

Despite being erotic and passionate, Leo enjoys being pursued. Sexually provocative, you turn on the sexual magnets and wait to see who is drawn in. Once you have caught your prey, megawatts are focused on the object of your affections. You have a strong sex drive and no hesitation in expressing this in torrid sex, but you may be only playing at love.

Leo says
'Adore me.'

What you seek
Love, hot sex, romance and excitement, fidelity and commitment, marriage, long-term security.

What turns you on

A Leo in love is permanently turned on. The ultimate aphrodisiac for this passionate sign is love and oodles of admiration. There is nothing you like more than to be the centre of attention. To arouse you your partner should stroke and knead your lower back – and not worry about sheathing those claws. A little pain is pleasurable to the fiery lion, provided it doesn't go too far.

You and your fantasy

Leo loves dressing up and enthusiastically participates in role play, so your fantasies are active, steamy and erotic. A dominatrix is a favourite, whether you are giving or receiving punishment. Most Leos are exhibitionists and you may fantasize about performing in front of an appreciative audience.

How you behave as a partner

It is important for your self-image to believe that you have someone special and you do not easily forgive mistakes. However, while partnership is important to you, Leo is not into equal partnership. You need to be the dominant one – although someone who is too subservient would soon become boring to you. You want a partner who responds to your passionate nature and, in return, you offer enduring love. You have a tendency to lionize your partner, wanting to both admire and know everything there is to know.

The fixed nature of your sign means that you stick with a relationship, especially marriage, although you may toy with the fantasy of other partners. You expect your partner to understand that, no matter how much you may respond to flirtatious overtures, you are simply indulging your ego and at heart you are loyal. Nevertheless Leo is not averse to playing away from home if you think you can get away with it. To you loyalty means not leaving – or, more importantly, not getting found out – rather than eternal faithfulness.

When you feel safe and secure with a partner you allow them into your inner world of fantasy and eroticism. Most Leos have a strong fantasy life and look for a playmate, someone to act out and enjoy those fantasies. Some of your fantasies involve bondage and allowing a partner to tie you up shows an enormous amount of trust on your part. You need a lover who appreciates, and never violates, that trust. Given that, you are a loyal and loving life-partner. Cultivating forgiveness, along with humility, could make your relationships run more smoothly.

What you expect from a partner

You demand fidelity, loyalty and fun. As you see your partner as a reflection of your own worth, your partner needs to look good all the time and your partner would be well advised to feign sleep until the ravages of the night have been repaired.

When it ends

Leo pride makes it almost certain that you leave rather than are left, but either way you hide your hurt pride beneath a dignified façade. You fight to the death to keep what you consider to be yours, and your partner has to pay dearly for the break-up. Leo is rarely able to shoulder the blame, insisting on being the innocent party in any divorce.

Leo relationships

Understanding your Leo man

A Leo man is proud – and vain: this is the man with big hair and huge gold belt buckle. Flatter him, praise him and pay him lots of attention. Be an engaging companion and indulge his passions; this man has boundless energy and hates to be bored. Above all else your Leo man needs to be admired so don't be surprised if you have to share him. Gregarious Leos have masses of friends of both sexes but, at the end of the day, his heart is with you and he is a loyal lover.

   This man needs someone at his side who looks good, but who doesn't take the lead – unless you're acting out a leonine fantasy that is. He wants his companion to be intelligent, engaging and highly stimulating, but not so much so that attention is diverted away from himself. If you manage this difficult balancing act, your reward is a warm-hearted, considerate lover who showers you with gifts.

   Underneath the outer assurance, your Leo man may be unsure: all those glances in the mirror, flicking back that hair, can mask a real fear that he is not good enough. That's why image is so important to him. A convincing actor, Leo finds it difficult to admit such feelings exist. He needs to be very sure of you before he unburdens himself. Betray his confidence at your cost: trust is important to Leo. He has an almost naive faith in people but, once let down, his pride will not allow him to risk being wrong again. You need to understand his pride. He hates being poked fun at, loathes making mistakes

Leo man

Passion rating
★★★★★

How to make it work

Let him take the lead, do not ignore him, and never, ever discuss his performance with your girl friends.

and fears being inadequate. His pride, like his will, is indomitable and intractable. Leo men don't bend easily and they certainly don't take orders. Try a little gentle persuasion; humour works wonders for this man. Appeal to his better nature and you'll soon have him eating out of the palm of your hand.

Understanding your Leo woman

An ebullient Leo woman is a lot like a Leo man. Sexually provocative, she is indefatigable in bed and needs to be the centre of attention. You would be wise not to let your eyes stray when you are with this predatory female, but will be expected to stand by placidly while she flirts and flatters your friends with sexual innuendo. She enjoys playing and wants to be entertained, amused and pampered but in return her generous heart pampers you and enfolds you in her sunny warmth.

You would be wise to remember that, no matter how playful she may be, your Leo woman has formidable pride. Under no circumstances does she want to look stupid, silly or undignified. And she always expects to take the lead.

Leo woman

Passion rating
★ ★ ★ ★ ★

How to make it work
Flatter her, adore her and let her be the boss.

Other relationships

Leo makes a wonderful friend. Open-hearted and generous, exuberant and larger-than-life, this sign loves to play but appreciates notice of an outing – because your friend needs time to dress up and look Leo's magnificent best. There is no better companion for a shopping spree, the opera or a party, as this self-indulgent sign enjoys good food, good wine and excellent conversation With Leo for a friend, be prepared to play sycophant to a Queen Bee. This gregarious sign craves adulation and flattery. It is most important to understand: *Leo needs attention*. You must be prepared to make your Leo friend the centre of your universe.

Leos are proud and it is easy to slight a Leo without knowing why. If your friend suddenly stands tall and looks distant, you have inadvertently transgressed. Did you tease or poke fun? Laugh at a minor mishap? Comment unfavourably on dress? Disagree? All are cardinal sins in Leo's eyes. Fortunately it doesn't take long for Leo *joie de vivre* to reinstate itself and Leos rarely hold grudges.

Leo is a drama junkie. Your friend demands that you listen, sympathize and agonize. Make sure Leo phones you; bills will be astronomical. Your Leo friend might listen to your troubles but, sooner rather than later, the spotlight switches back to Leo. Nevertheless, this sign can be ferocious in defending those it loves.

When something, or someone, more exciting intervenes, Leo exits without a backward glance. There are gaps in a Leo friendship: it picks up where Leo left it, when Leo is ready. But your Leo chum is worth waiting for. This is a loyal, funny and kind-hearted ally. Leo provides a friend without malice, someone to treasure.

Leo wants a warm working environment, but one that is dominated by Leo. Leo quickly gets personal, and you may well find your Leo co-worker flirting with you and there can be a strong sexual undertone at work. Ignore this at your peril as if Leo feels slighted, things can get frosty. But, on the other hand, don't take it too seriously. If you remember the Leo pride and the need to be admired, your working relationship runs smoothly and inevitably spills over into your personal life. Leo's generous hospitality invariably includes co-workers as friends.

Where things get problematic is when Leo becomes competitive. This domineering sign is into power plays in a big way and can be surprisingly manipulative, using friendship and intimacy as ploys to gain control. Remember that if friendly persuasion doesn't work Leo can become a despotic dictator.

Compatibility chart

Aries ★ ★ ★ ★

Taurus ★ ★ ★

Gemini ★ ★ ★

Cancer ★

Leo ★ ★

Virgo ★ ★

Libra ★ ★ ★ ★ ★

Scorpio ★ ★ ★ ★

Sagittarius ★ ★ ★ ★ ★

Capricorn ★ ★

Aquarius ★ ★ ★ ★ ★

Pisces ★ ★

Virgo
the virgin

23 August – 22 September
Passive • Mutable • Earth

Virgo is the quietly sexy sign of the zodiac; discreet flirtation is one of your hobbies. Witty and well-informed, you have refined verbal foreplay into an art. You can appear quite prim on the surface but underneath you have strong carnal desires and your natural sensuality means that you are highly responsive when aroused. Setting exacting standards for your lovers, who have to be aesthetically pleasing as well as demonstrating sexual prowess, mental rapport is important and you want an intelligent companion for life. With analytic Mercury as your ruler, you have an unquenchable curiosity which is applied to all things sexual. Until you find your life partner, you are content to play the field and enjoy sensual exploration. Picky and discriminating, you know exactly what does, or does not, turn you on, and are into the rituals of courtship and romance.

What makes you tick: finessing your way into love

First appearances are deceptive with Virgo. You appear to be communicating freely and openly but perceptive partners may notice that, as the relationship progresses, they learn little more that is new or deeply meaningful. There is an intimacy point beyond which you do not venture. This is because, as a pragmatic earth sign ruled by cerebral Mercury, you are cut off from your deepest feelings which, therefore, you cannot express.

Yours is a perfectionist sign: you are driven by high ideals and standards that are almost impossible to meet. With a powerful inner critic at work, it is difficult for your partner to avoid being criticized for failing to meet these expectations and you are aware of every little flaw.

However, you criticize yourself just as much as your partner. It would be helpful to ease up as you are prone to psychosomatic ailments in response to self-induced stress.

Your style

Cool, chatty and reliable; efficient, hard-working and co-operative.

A fastidious sign with an earthy urge towards promiscuity, you like to talk about sex, and you enjoy looking at bodies, but the messy business of the sex act itself can be a turn-off for you. Yours is not a sign that gets carried away by passion, or by sentiment: you want to be in charge of your body but at the same time you need to express your earthy sexuality. For you this is best done within a relationship with someone you trust, someone who is on the same mental wavelength but who can stoke the fires of your carefully managed lust.

Virgo is a sign that likes to serve others but which can so easily slip into servitude or servility instead. Partners would do well to acknowledge and appreciate all that is done for them by this willing slave as otherwise Virgo becomes depressed.

Your relationship style

Your sexual style is one of cool ardour rather than ardent passion and you show love by doing things for your partner. Being a pernickety sign, it takes you quite a while to commit, but once you have made that choice, you tend to be faithful, although in time you may drift into platonic friendship as you value mental rapport rather more than sexual compatibility. If this occurs you may have the occasional discreet fling but you do hesitate to leave the long-term security of your primary relationship as your home and family mean a great deal to you.

Virgo says
'Is it perfect?'

What you seek
Sensuality, love, commitment; a long-term companion.

Your seduction technique

Your unruffled surface shows little of the earthy sensual passion of which you are capable as you reserve that for private, intimate moments. As with everything your search for perfection leads you to be cautious when it comes to a possible partner, so you approach things very slowly and then seduce with well-chosen words.

What turns you on

For fastidious Virgo the mind and the skin are erogenous and an aesthetically pleasing nude arouses your lust. Nibbling your fingers and toes is exciting, and some Virgos have a foot fetish, eroticizing freshly painted toe nails and shapely feet. But you are also turned on by soap and water and your nose is an important part of your lovemaking. By way of a change, you may find yourself turned on by ripe sexual odours, or by pornography.

You and your fantasy

Your most vivid fantasies take place in your inventive mind and read like a porn script. There is the nurse's uniform and the trolley the rubber gloves and the shower; or the mud-wrestling lesbians; or ... Many need a large cast and most are all about things you would never dare to do in real life! When you do act out your fantasies, they may well take place in the bathroom.

How you behave as a partner

Virgo is extremely courteous and considerate but partners can expect cool displays of affection, especially in public, as you reserve your passion for the bedroom. However, you are responsive to overtures by your partner and your underlying sensuality can soon be brought to the surface, especially by a romantic gesture.

Trust and intimacy
Cautious trust, superficial intimacy.

Secret sexual desire
Starring in a porn movie.

Yours is a discriminating sign that values quality and does not indulge in extravagance and so you tend not to shower your partner with gifts. You prefer to perform a service of some kind, no matter how small, to indicate 'I love you.'

While earthy Virgo is naturally faithful, you belong to a mutable sign and these signs have a tendency to play outside marriage. With your witty repartee and discreetly flirtatious nature, you may well attract sexual attention, and are unlikely to resist the opportunity for a quiet fling.

One of the trickiest things for your partner to handle is your tendency to nit-pick, and your insistence on doing everything to an exceptionally high standard. You can drive your partner to distraction if you are not careful. With your gift of analysis, you examine every detail. If you feel that something could have been done better, or that more work could have gone into it, you do not hesitate to say so. As a result your partner feels criticized even when you did not mean to criticize.

What you expect from a partner

You expect your partner to be faithful, although you may forgive the occasional fling. With your need for intellectual companionship, you want a partner who is on your mental wavelength and who has the same standards and ideals as yourself. You would find it difficult to live with anyone who was dirty or untidy in their personal habits, and appreciate a partner who is an excellent host or hostess for the intimate gatherings you so carefully plan.

When it ends

Virgo is rather civilized about endings. Things do not happen suddenly. You slowly realize that your partner has become your platonic friend, and eventually one or other of you finds a new partner, but you may still holiday together for the sake of the children. Separation is easier for you than divorce, as this is acknowledging a mistake in your eyes; but when it is finally over, you want things to be tidy and ensure that all the legal matters are taken care of fairly.

Virgo relationships

Understanding your Virgo man

All you need to know to understand this modest and refined man is that he is seeking perfection and much of his time is spent analyzing his behaviour to see whether or not he could have been better. So if he looks a little distracted after sex, he is probably reviewing his performance and giving himself marks out of ten. His inner critic probably allocates a low mark so you could boost your man's ego by offering praise.

He lives constantly with this nagging and insistent inner critic – it never lets up. If he can learn to put this on one side and loosen up, he is a much happier man. But it is a huge task for him. His natural inclination is to look at all the fine detail, to take things to pieces, extract the essence, and then see how it measures up. The goals he sets himself are impossibly high, as are the standards he tries to meet. The problem is he applies those same standards to everyone else so you have to measure up too.

Aside from his desire for perfection, he also has to contend with an earthy, lusty nature. He wants to be sensuous and sexy, but again the critic comes in, this time wearing his inner prude hat, and your Virgo man might retreat into a psychosomatic ailment in response. Virgo is health conscious, and reacts physically to mental or emotional stress. If you can make a game out of

Virgo man

Passion rating
★ ★ ★ ✦

How to make it work
Live up to his ideals.

his inner prude, consigning it to the wardrobe for the duration of your lovemaking, for example, your Virgo man will be a much more inventive and enthusiastic lover.

Understanding your Virgo woman

A Virgo woman is more comfortable with her sexuality than a Virgo man. She has the same high ideals and that nagging inner critic, but somehow she can silence her urge for perfection and live in the moment, throwing her inhibitions to the wind. She has a deep desire to be helpful, and to be needed: some of what she does for others boosts her own sense of self-worth. But on the whole she performs these services because that is part of her nature and appreciation is a bonus she cherishes but can live without.

Virgo woman

Passion rating
★ ★ ★ ★

How to make it work
Never clutter the place up and be scrupulous in your personal hygiene.

Other relationships

If all goes well between you, your Virgo friend is great fun to be around. He or she probably prefers small intimate gatherings to large crowds, but this is an excellent companion for music or theatre trips, the gym, walks in the country or a visit to a health farm. Virgo is full of practical advice, and is a very handy person to be available if your house needs redecoration or repairs. Your Virgo friend is pretty solid in an emotional crisis too, although the crisis is analyzed meticulously afterwards. This is someone you can trust, someone you can share your secrets with – as long as you remember to extract a promise that they remain a secret. This sign is ruled by Mercury after all, and he is a chatty kind of chap.

If things go wrong it is because your Virgo friend is applying his or her terribly high standards and is finding you wanting in some way. If so, ask. Virgo is happy to discuss it and might even laugh when the inventory of faults comes to an end and he or she sees the absurdity of it.

Fortunately Virgo has an excellent sense of humour and this witty sign has the ability to laugh at itself as well as others. If you want to be entertained with intelligence, phone your Virgo friend.

As a co-worker Virgo makes a great one, enjoying mutual projects and being naturally co-operative. This sign is detail-oriented and focuses on what is relevant at that moment, so your co-worker is adept at getting to the crux of the matter. This is a natural problem solver who is able to create the highest quality with minimum resources. A workaholic, Virgo's motto is that if a job's worth doing, it's worth doing to perfection. This exacting attitude means that Virgo quickly becomes indispensable. This is the person you go to when you need facts and figures: the detail is immaculate and the data reliably sourced.

However, remember that your Virgo co-worker is a workaholic who can drive him- or herself too hard. This sign always feels that there is something more to do and, unless swept out of work for a drink, burns the midnight oil with resulting stress. Your Virgo co-worker is something of a hypochondriac and has every remedy going for whatever ails, or is likely to ail, you. The most thoughtful thing you can do is ask after your Virgo co-worker's health, sympathize, and then get on with your own work. Virgo does the same.

Compatibility chart

Aries ★	Libra ★
Taurus ★★★★★	Scorpio ★★★
Gemini ★	Sagittarius ★★★
Cancer ★★★★	Capricorn ★★★★★
Leo ★	Aquarius ★★★
Virgo ★★★★★	Pisces ★★★★★

Libra
the scales

23 September – 23 October
Active • Cardinal • Air

You have been blessed with sexual charisma and gentle charm. In love with love, flirtatious Libra has an innate ability to relate to everyone, making each one feel the centre of your world. Relationships make you feel complete and you prefer being one half of a couple to independent solitude. You want to find a soul mate and the whole business of romance is essential for you. Taking delight in appeasing and pleasing, you adapt to your partner so your relationships are always harmonious. You may compromise so much that you lose sight of your own needs and eventually these surface with great force. At that point partners may discover that Libra is not quite such a nice sign after all, but you are too peace-loving to allow that state of affairs to continue long, especially as you yearn for marital bliss.

What makes you tick: charming your way into love

Partnerships are what make you feel complete. A people pleaser at heart, everything you do is oriented towards creating a harmonious relationship and your desire for peace at all costs may mean that you compromise to a point where you lose sight of yourself and your values. Togetherness is what life is about for you and you intuitively respond to people's needs, putting your own on hold. Eventually these needs make themselves known, forcefully.

Libra is renowned for being a diplomatic but indecisive sign, but this is not strictly true. Yes, you find decisions difficult and choices confusing, but this is because you see everything from several different perspectives and need time to weigh up the pros and cons. Once you have made your decision, you stick with it, unless someone offers you another, more compelling, view.

> **Your style**
> Thoughtful, caring and extremely co-operative; goes all out for a harmonious working environment.

What most people don't understand is that you are searching for perfection. You want to look good, you need a pleasing ambiance and you dream of a perfect relationship. Which may lead you to judge people on appearance rather than inner qualities. The cardinal side of your nature emerges when you have to make one compromise too many; you have standards below which you do not go. People who view you as a pushover are surprised when you suddenly dig in your heels. This is the moment when they understand that your extremely nice façade disguises a tough interior.

Your relationship style

Relationships are extremely important to you and so you work at them, taking care not to conflict with your partner. You are capable of putting your sexual needs or desires on hold, or switching them on, in order to please or accommodate your lover. Flirtatious and sociable, you like to have people around but usually remain loyal. However, you are capable of having a discreet affair to take care of your own carnal desires.

Your seduction technique

Slinky and seductive, flirtatious Libra is laid-back but determined. You prefer allurement and guile to blatant pursuit but you get your man, or woman, through charm, or bewitchment if necessary. Simply by focusing all your attention on a prospective partner, you lure them into your arms.

What turns you on

You appreciate the rituals of courtship and love to be wooed with sophistication and finesse. Your erogenous zones are the buttocks, and kneading or gentle slapping and pinching excite you. To hear your lover whispering flattering sweet nothings in your ear is a joy to you. Your sign was made for pleasure but the setting has to be right, nothing tacky or messy, and your senses need to be aroused by sensual perfume and silken fabrics.

You and your fantasy

Libra lives a lifelong fantasy of romance and courtship, spending hours dreaming about an ideal lover (even when married). The details may be hazy and the action in soft focus but the overall idea is a beautiful lover who sweeps you off to a romantic destination and who worships and pleasures only you. The darker side of your fantasies may include all those things you would never normally voice, expressing your darkly erotic desires, and many centre around giving or receiving forbidden pleasure. Occasionally you may act these out with a partner you trust implicitly or you may find yourself acting out your partner's fantasies instead.

How you behave as a partner

Sociable and romantic, you enjoy snuggling up with a partner but, in public at least, you can focus your attention on someone else for a while. Although you appear to be totally absorbed in that person, you expect your partner to know that you are not being disloyal, you are simply interested in people and enjoying the conversation. When it is time to leave, you happily return to your partner and would not understand a sulky or angry reaction to your interest in others, although you would do everything you could to smooth things over. One of your delights is choosing exactly the right gift for your partner, especially as a peace offering.

Trust and intimacy
Totally trusting, intimacy personified.

Secret sexual desire
Ravishment.

It is as a partner that Libra's need to please is most noticeable. You put your partner first in everything, adapting and adjusting to every whim. As a result you lack authenticity: the real you has become lost in what your partner wants you to be. At some point in your life, you have to rediscover who you are.

Although marriage is not vitally important to you, commitment is. You want to be seen to be in a solid partnership; after all appearances matter to you. The security of a lifelong bond makes you feel comfortable with your life and few Libras feel fulfilled by a life that does not include a relationship.

What you expect from a partner

Libra wants fidelity and faithfulness, but your ability to compromise means that you may accept a partner's tendency to stray, or subconsciously expect it. Your natural instinct is to make allowances, and to apologize for your lack of whatever it is you think is missing from your relationship. This is particularly so if your desire for a relationship at any cost has won out over your desire for perfection. Somehow you blame yourself for everything that goes wrong rather than ending an unsatisfactory liaison. You leave that to your partner to do.

When it ends

Being a Libra if you left you probably had another partner waiting. Hating confrontation, you want to be terribly fair and find it hard to apportion blame. You invariably apologize to everyone concerned. There are no arguments, things are divided up equally, and matters are tended to with a minimum of fuss. Nevertheless a break-up hits you hard and you need time to grieve.

Libra relationships

Understanding your Libra man

Suave, charming, impeccably groomed, and eminently fanciable, your Libra man winds you round his little finger while professing that your happiness is all he cares about. Subtle manipulation is one of the ploys he uses to ensure he gets the best possible relationship with the least hassle. Not that you'll mind – he is such pleasant company and so romantic that you willingly fall into his trap. This winsome man adjusts to your needs, never argues nor makes demands, provides sex whenever you want it and romances you forever. Until, that is, it inconveniences him. Under that nice façade there is a selfish, lazy streak and a stubborn one. He cannot be coerced. This man makes promises, but won't always keep them, and is a master of little white lies that avoid his having to hurt your feelings. He'd rather tell a white lie than face an argument. His comfort zone is important to him, and he won't put himself out.

The ambiance of his home is important; he is physically uncomfortable with dirt, mess and clashing colours. He expects you to keep his house beautifully and needs you to look good, and delights in helping you to find exactly the right clothes. This is a man who enjoys retail therapy and who can be extravagant when buying something he values, but a surprisingly mean streak can emerge.

Libra man

Passion rating
★ ★ ★

How to make it work
Don't argue with him, don't nag, and don't leave the decisions up to him.

Understanding your Libra woman

As you will have discovered, your Libra woman is alluring and eminently beddable, and she longs to please you. This is a woman with an enormous sense of style. What you may not have discovered is that her appearance matters a great deal to her and she would prefer you not to disarray her carefully arranged hair or rumple her immaculate clothing, even in the most passionate clinch.

Be gentle around her or you may meet the steely, hidden side of Libra that wants things all her own way. This woman is tough and uncompromising, once she makes up her mind. It is not that she is indecisive, it is more that she sees all sides and wants to be fair. She has a passion for perfection, and although she makes many compromises to achieve personal harmony, in the end she wants things to be *right*.

Libra woman

Passion rating
★ ★ ★

How to make it work
Don't confuse her with choices; flatter her; take her on shopping trips; create a harmonious atmosphere; and never complain when she is late.

Other relationships

What your sociable Libra friend is seeking is harmony. If he, or she, finds that you are attuned to the same things, you have a friend for life. This cultured soul enjoys the arts and aesthetics, good food and excellent company: you can party together or have intimate dinners to discuss your deepest feelings.

Libra is into sharing emotions in a big way. This is a friend who may enter into a polite debate with you, but who is unlikely to fight over anything, preferring to end the friendship rather than disagree. Your friend belongs to a sign that keeps the peace no matter what and can calm even the most argumentative of signs.

However, you need to know that this does not make your Libra friend the most truthful person in your life. You are told what you want to hear, or what your friend thinks you want to hear. Anything that might cause you pain is skirted around; if it's plain, unvarnished truth you are seeking, look elsewhere. If it's advice you need though, Libra is extremely helpful. You are shown all sides of the picture, and given all the options. Just don't expect your Libra friend to make the decision for you.

A word of warning. Libra is a terrible timekeeper and you should make allowances for this. Almost inevitably late, your Libra friend still can't resist looking in the mirror. This sign can take hours in the bathroom; Libra simply has to look good. The hair is combed, clothes smoothed, make-up reapplied in front of each and every mirror. Your Libra friend's grooming consumes hours of your time.

Libra is a skilled team builder and loves to be a co-worker. This is the person who ensures harmony reigns in the workplace, and who applies all those finishing touches that make it a comfortable place to be. Libra's diplomatic skills smooth over any ruffled feelings or points of disagreement and life flows wonderfully smoothly. Until you ask your Libra colleague to make a decision. Libra gathers in all the facts and figures and calls endless meetings so that he or she can go over every aspect, as Libra looks at it first one way and then another.

If you are wise you keep your Libra co-worker out of the decision-making loop by presenting the finished product and asking how it can be improved: don't offer this or that choices. This allows your Libra co-worker to do what he or she does best – add the final flourish that makes the product superb.

Compatibility chart

Aries ★ ★ ★ ★ ★	Libra ★ ★ ★ ★ ★
Taurus ★ ★ ★	Scorpio ★ ★
Gemini ★ ★	Sagittarius ★ ★ ★ ★ ★
Cancer ★	Capricorn ★ ★ ★
Leo ★ ★ ★ ★ ★	Aquarius ★ ★ ★
Virgo ★ ★	Pisces ★ ★ ★

Scorpio

the scorpion

24 October – 21 November
Passive • Fixed • Water

One of the most sexually intense signs, Scorpio's sexual stamina is legendary, as is your talent for seduction. Magnetic and charismatic, you have a libido that runs deep and strong although little shows on the surface. 'Still waters run deep' perfectly describes your personality. Intensely private and protective of your own feelings, your fear of being controlled holds you back from surrendering fully to the dance of love, although some of your sexual encounters are mystical in their intensity. Enigmatic and unfathomable, you say more with silence than other signs do with words: powerful emotional currents run through your inner being. Compulsive in your search for sexual gratification, you can be manipulative and forceful in pursuit of a love object. You rarely confuse lust with love and your red-hot passion burns as brightly for a passing fling as it does for the love of a lifetime.

What makes you tick: powering your way into love

It is virtually impossible to know what makes a Scorpio tick – mystery and intrigue are part of your charisma. Getting to know you is an enormous challenge but one that your immensely sexy persona can make almost irresistible. You are compulsively secretive, pathologically cautious, strictly controlling and emotionally defensive, and that is only for starters. Your inner self is protected by the infamous Scorpio sting. Gentle and tender signs would do well to steer clear!

On the other hand you are a water sign and long for intimacy and emotional melding. It takes time for you to trust, but when you do you give your all to your partner. If that trust is broken, it is a very long time indeed before you trust again. If your jealousy is triggered, your partner had better watch out: the Scorpio sting can be lethal.

Your inner self is a lot less confident than your outer façade would suggest, which is why you protect yourself so well. You need other people and, as a result, you feel emotionally vulnerable, especially when in the grip of the obsessional emotional tides that sweep through your inner being. Control is important to you, both of your emotions and your environment.

Letting go of the past is a challenge: you tend to pre-judge the present in the light of your past pain. Letting go would be beneficial. There are times when Scorpio appears to have a death wish; you have a compulsive need to explore all that is hidden and forbidden.

Your style
Intense, secretive, loyal and hard-working.

Your relationship style
You are a seductive lover who knows exactly how to turn a partner on but who keeps personal desires strictly under wraps and who can be emotionally insensitive. Once you do succumb to love rather than lust,

you are an exceedingly loyal partner but may expect your partner to act out some of your darker sexual urges. When you enter into a committed relationship, you are slow to reveal your intensely emotional self. With your obsessive nature you spend a great deal of time fantasizing about your beloved and keep a jealous watch on your partner's activities.

Your seduction technique

Scorpio has enormous magnetism and your sexual pull is irresistible. Your amorous intensity smoulders beneath the surface, its force being felt rather than seen. When you seduce you size up the carnal potential, move in slowly, turn on your magnets, and await results. Once aroused, however, you are capable of forcing sex upon someone by overwhelming them with passion, and it may well be a fleeting lust.

> **Scorpio says**
> Very little!
>
> **What you seek**
> Erotic sex; power, marriage, commitment and loyalty.

What turns you on

Scorpio's erogenous zones are the organs of procreation and the anus and perineum. Stimulation of these areas is greatly arousing for you, as is sensual massage on any part of your body. Your sign finds pleasure in pain, and sadomasochism can be a major turn-on for you, whether as voyeur or participant.

You and your fantasy

Scorpio fantasies tend to be darkly erotic, hidden and forbidden, featuring sexual slavery, dominance and black leather. Sadistic figures such as Miss or Mr Whiplash make their appearance, and may be played out, but your most erotic fantasies occur only in your mind as this allows you to explore the taboos that hold such a compulsive fascination for you.

Your planetary ruler, the powerful Pluto, was associated with abduction and rape and you may well fantasize coming under the spell of his sexual mastery, or of wielding such power yourself.

How you behave as a partner

Scorpio can be very intense about partnership. Much as you would like to be emotionally self-sufficient, you need other people and there are times when you create an almost mystical connection with your partner.

That does not mean, however, that you share yourself fully in your relationship. You are innately secretive, something is always held back and perceptive partners are aware of this. It would be helpful if you would open up, but it is against your nature to do so and partners need to tread gently with you. They also need to be aware that they are not immune from your sting.

Although you are loyal, you may well not be faithful. To you these two things are entirely different. You revel in swift flings and torrid but unemotional sex. If you are not getting enough sexual excitement, you fantasize in your head about other partners, and cannot understand why your partner would object to this emotional unfaithfulness. However, Scorpio is one of the most jealous and possessive of the zodiac signs and you do not allow your partner the same freedom.

Trust and intimacy
Deeply suspicious, little intimacy.

Secret sexual desire
Autoeroticism.

What you expect from a partner

You expect a depth of loyalty from your partner that matches your own, and an intensity of passion that meets your powerfully erotic sexual needs whenever and however they arise. While you value a partner who understands your moods, you shy away from one who knows too many of the secrets of your heart and you want a partner who does not intrude on the innermost parts of yourself.

When it ends

Scorpio is highly resistant to change and does not like endings. If your partner is leaving, love quickly turns to spite and you make things as difficult as possible especially with your barbed tongue. If you are leaving, while a feeling of guilt may make you promise the world, you still want to hold on to your assets at all costs and you take an exceedingly long time to let go.

Scorpio relationships

Understanding your Scorpio man

Deeply secretive, a Scorpio man won't reveal himself voluntarily, and you need to tread warily in seeking insights that don't make him feel you are invading his privacy. Once he knows that you know, however, he is much relieved. He, of course, has already sussed out everything about you. He can see into your very soul and there is no protecting yourself. Finding it incredibly difficult to trust, his tongue can be lethal – and he knows all your weak spots. Unless you relish being seduced and laid bare do not contemplate relationship with a Scorpio.

This inscrutable man is one of the most complex and darkly emotional in the zodiac; his nature partakes of the scorpion. He hides, he skulks, and then he stings you without warning and for no reason. On the other hand he can be charming, charismatic, magnetic and very, very sexy. It all depends on his mood: one moment he is brooding and totally insensitive to your feelings, the next he is a considerate lover who subtly manipulates you where he wants to go.

And this seductive man has an urge to go where other signs fear to tread and to explore all that is taboo and hidden. He simply cannot live on the surface of life. At times it seems like he has a death wish but at others he takes you into the depths of a mystical emotional connection. His carnal urges are powerful but his control is tight. One of his strongest lessons in life is to master the enormous power that smoulders inside him without blowing others away in the process.

The Scorpio world can be one of paranoid fears, compulsions and powerful addictions – of which sex can be the strongest. Despite an outward appearance of confidence, your

> ### Scorpio man
>
> **Passion rating**
> ★★★★★
>
> **How to make it work**
> Understand his need for secrecy and control.

Scorpio man is deeply insecure. If you accept this you help him come to terms with the blackest part of himself. Scorpio is enormously courageous and shining a light into the darkness brings to light the Plutonian richness of this enigmatic sign.

Understanding your Scorpio woman

This torrid and tantalizing female has much in common with Scorpio man. They share the same intensity, the same magnetism and the same need for secrecy. She too can sting you without warning, especially when she perceives there is danger, and her insecurity takes you into some dark emotional spaces. But she is fiercely loyal and highly erotic. If you allow her the private interior space she needs, and recognize that intimacy is hard for her, she learns to trust you. Once you have gained her trust, you have her love and she introduces you to the dark fantasies and fears of her interior world, and the obsessions and compulsions that rule her life. Embrace them, and she is yours forever.

Scorpio woman

Passion rating
★ ★ ★ ★ ★

How to make it work
Remember that she likes to dominate.

Other relationships

Anyone who has anything to do with Scorpio needs to know about the Scorpio sting in the tail. Don't invite comment unless you are well-defended yourself. Scorpios can't help it – they lash out verbally without warning even if you haven't done anything to offend them. It is their nature so don't take it personally. If you have said something to upset their sensitive soul, beware – a tongue-lashing definitely follows. And there isn't much you can do to circumvent this.

Understanding your Scorpio friend is easier than understanding your Scorpio lover because this sign does not feel as exposed by friendship as by love. Your friend, in time, shares deep feelings with you and this sign has powerful insights into all matters hidden and forbidden. You may well find that, when the friendship has matured, you are honoured with confessions of Scorpio's previously untold secrets. This sign has journeyed into the underworld and you may find the secrets shocking. But if you show this, your Scorpio friend withdraws and you will not regain that trust. The secrets may be something which your Scorpio friend fears offend, but if you can provide reassurance that they are perfectly natural, you can relieve some of that deep Scorpio guilt and help Scorpio to lighten up a bit. When it comes to telling your own secrets, you won't have to! Everything is laid bare to Scorpio's penetrating gaze before you unburden yourself. There is little that shocks or surprises this sign and you can find profound emotional support during the traumas and dramas of your life, and some sage advice on how to meet your challenges.

Your Scorpio friend has a fun side too and many Scorpios take partying very seriously indeed. This is the original sex, drugs and rock'n'roll sign but your Scorpio friend likes sophisticated entertainment too, and clubbing. An ideal companion for a murder mystery weekend, your Scorpio friend particularly likes ferreting out secrets but may channel this into tarot readings and the like. This is a sign that has a deep connection to metaphysics.

Your Scorpio co-worker is almost certainly inscrutable, and something of a control freak, but is also hard-working and conscientious. Scorpio dislikes change so it is unwise to rush in with revolutionary ideas; they need to be introduced gradually. Your Scorpio co-worker is not given to warning you as you approach dodgy ground; the first you know about it is when that sting lands. But one thing you can rely on is loyal support.

Compatibility chart

Aries ★★★★

Taurus ★★★★★

Gemini ★★

Cancer ★★★★

Leo ★★★★

Virgo ★★

Libra ★★

Scorpio ★★★

Sagittarius ★

Capricorn ★★★

Aquarius ★★★★

Pisces ★★★★★

Sagittarius
the archer

22 November – 21 December
Active • Mutable • Fire

Sagittarius is a free spirit who roams the world in search of adventure. Your attitude to relationships is casual, you'll happily have a quick fling, or a mad, passionate affair that lasts months; you might move in with your lover as long as there is tempestuous sex, but eventually you'll want to move on. Marriage is not your ideal state. For Sagittarius the grass is always greener somewhere else and you are never quite convinced that you have found your life-partner. A romantic at heart, and someone who spontaneously shows affection, you often think you have found true love only to find that you have confused it with a passing lust. Happiest with a partner who allows you the space you need, and who is delighted to pack a suitcase and accompany you on your latest trip, you seldom travel alone for long.

What makes you tick: insouciantly falling into love

Yours is a happy-go-lucky, uncomplicated sign and 'what you see is what you get'. You are straightforward in your dealings with people, preferring truth and openness. A naturally trusting and optimistic person, you have faith in everyone – until you discover differently – but you hate being lied to. If someone does lie, although you may give them a second chance, you never totally trust them. Renowned for being a tactless sign, you tell it like it is. Not for you white lies that avoid hurt, you say things bluntly and don't bother to wrap it up. Until that is there is something you'd rather your partner didn't know – Sagittarius can then be somewhat shy with the truth but, not being a good liar, it is impossible to keep up a pretence and ultimately the truth will out. When it does your partner should not expect apologies: Sagittarius moves smartly on.

'Never explain and never apologize' is your credo and you rarely look back with regret. Spontaneous and active, you have an insatiable need to know and pursue this relentlessly, which is why you value your freedom so highly. While you are happy to stay voluntarily, the thought of being tied down to one person is extremely difficult. Wise partners give you lots of space. They recognize that even the most exciting plans become boring to you if they have been made too far in advance. You much prefer to fire all your arrows in the air at once and see where that takes you.

Your style

Gregarious, bright, breezy, spontaneous, hard-working but not too dedicated.

Most Sagittarians have lofty ideals. You need something to inspire you and something to believe in and you prefer to share this with your partner but can go it alone. Given a cause you can become fanatical and give your all but you have a tendency to promise more than you can deliver, from the best of motives of course.

Your relationship style

You seek a partner who understands and shares your need for freedom and adventure. Given sufficient space you can be a committed and caring partner, albeit one who finds the state of matrimony difficult. If you find yourself trapped, you leave, but you can be a loyal partner who freely forgives foibles and lapses on the part of others provided that you have not been lied to.

Your seduction technique

Sagittarius is an adventurous sign, enjoying the thrill of the chase as much as the hot sex that follows. If someone plays too hard to get, you simply move on to the next possibility. Impulsive and feisty, you often confuse love with infatuation, and have sexual encounters for fun and friendship as well as lust.

What turns you on

Sagittarius is associated with hips and thighs and lightly stroking your inner thigh from knee to groin quickly inflames your erogenous zone. You find pursuing rather than being pursued a turn-on, especially if this takes place in the great outdoors; and Sagittarius always values an enthusiastic companion, shared ideas being hugely exciting.

You and your fantasy

The classic Sagittarius fantasy centres around horses and stables, but not all Sagittarians favour muck and straw; many prefer something out of the Arabian nights. Breakfast at the Ritz, lunch at Cipriani's, tea at Betty's Teashop, dinner on a tropical beach, with sex throughout, is an ever-present fantasy and one that is likely to get acted out. You prefer action to sex in your head.

How you behave as a partner

Sagittarius is a romantic at heart. Enjoying the trappings of courtship, you surprise your lover with presents or spur-of-the-moment outings. You forget to consult your lover's diary first, expecting him or her to drop whatever plans they had made to be with you. If there are objections you cannot understand why. After all life is for living, isn't it? If your partner turns the tables on you, you gladly go along with their surprise, provided you haven't anything more interesting in mind. You are not likely to put your own life on hold to fit into your partner's.

Your happy-go-lucky nature extends into your partnership arrangements and some signs see you as lacking in responsibility. If your partner asks you to do the shopping, you forget the staples and bring home the goodies. You would much rather your partner took over dull routine tasks, such as bill-paying, leaving you to enjoy the fun part of your relationship. You want to have a good time but your generous nature wants your partner to have a good time too. You are the kind of parent who takes your family on a round-the-world trip, totally unplanned naturally. But, somehow, you get away with it, for it will be wonderful experience for everyone.

What you expect from a partner

You need your partner to communicate with you: a strong silent type drives you to distraction. If you can't discuss things, you lose your vitality. You need a partner who also allows you freedom to roam; being kept on a short reign brings out the worst in you. Twenty-four-hour togetherness is not your style. It's not that you want to be unfaithful, just that you need to explore other possibilities and to have time for your hobbies and friends. That way, when you come back to the relationship, your interest is renewed.

When it ends

Before a relationship ends conclusively you have probably breathed a sigh of relief and left. As far as you are concerned, that is that. It only remains to tie up the legal niceties, and you're none too bothered about those. A Sagittarius is quite capable of walking out with nothing and starting from scratch – again.

Sagittarius relationships

Understanding your Sagittarius man

What you most need to know about your Sagittarius man is that he will not be tied down. Domesticity is not his bag, although if you give him freedom he happily stays around, and he might do the washing up. He is much more likely to take on chores if he thinks it was his idea.

Your Sagittarius man is frank and tactless. If you belong to one of the sensitive signs, remember that he is not trying to hurt you, he is telling it like it is. If you ask: 'Does my bum look big in this?' be prepared for an uncompromising 'Yes!' If the answer you get is 'No', then it's true. You can rely on your man to be truthful, unless he has something to hide. If he does you'll probably know: Sagittarius is an incompetent liar. The body language gives it away, that and the fact that your man inevitably lets it out in one of those foot-in-mouth moments he is prone to.

This man needs to debate and query and enquire. Sagittarius is the eternal student, whether of love, philosophy or material facts. What keeps your man a lively and entertaining companion is the opportunity to explore new things. This means that activities are taken up with great enthusiasm, only to be dropped again – so don't comment! It also means that your sociable Sagittarius man has a huge circle of 'pals', good friends of both sexes with whom he can enjoy life but who do not make emotional demands on him. A Sagittarius man cannot understand jealousy so a wise partner accepts that there are times when his companion is a woman, or man if yours is a same-sex relationship, but that doesn't necessarily mean sex is involved. It could – Sagittarius is not averse to sex with friends – but as long as you don't demand fidelity, he will probably be faithful.

Sagittarius man

Passion rating

★★★★

How to make it work

Improvise, give him plenty of space, join his adventures and be a stimulating companion on life's journey.

The most important thing to remember about your Sagittarius man is that he cannot tolerate boredom. This sign becomes positively lethal when mired in routine, so plan some surprises to keep your relationship fresh and lively.

Understanding your Sagittarius woman

A Sagittarius woman wants the same freedom as her male counterpart. Easily bored and, in some cases, competitive, she tends to use sport or outdoor activities to mop up her excess energy; but there are times when she wants to release this in the bedroom. At such times she needs raw sex without too many preliminaries; in another mood she wants to be wooed romantically. But you won't have to worry, she'll make her demands abundantly clear. This is a lady who knows her own mind.

Sagittarius woman

Passion rating

★ ★ ★ ★

How to make it work

Give her plenty of space, join her adventures and be a stimulating companion on life's journey.

Other relationships

Sagittarius makes a great friend. Gregarious, endlessly curious and enthusiastic, and very, very lively, he or she parties the night away, debates into the small hours, has long lunches or jumps on a plane with you. The spending capacity of this sign is legendary so this is just the person for a spot of retail therapy, if there is room on your credit card. Your Sagittarius friend won't even check the balance on theirs. The same applies when it's time to take a holiday: Sagittarius ups and goes. This intrepid traveller is delighted to take you along and you are guaranteed to boldly go where no tourist has been before.

You'll probably find you are part of a crowd; Sagittarius likes to be surrounded by mates and enjoys team sports. This ensures boredom is kept at bay. Your friend always has an opinion to air, so you'd better be ready with some comments of your own.

When it comes to a crisis, resourceful Sagittarius is useful to have on hand. The advice is sage, if sometimes somewhat impractical, and this is not a sign who panics easily. If your angst is emotional, your Sagittarius friend spends hours discussing all the intimate details; this sign is fascinated by what makes other people tick. However, if you want to keep your business private, swear Sagittarius to secrecy. This sign can be a bit of a blabbermouth. And one thing you can be sure to get from your Sagittarius friend is total honesty.

Sagittarius is a gregarious co-worker. Colleagues are inevitably assimilated into Sagittarius' large circle of friends and the boundaries between work and social life blur. Your Sagittarius co-worker rarely keeps personal matters to him- or herself. You share all the joys and problems of your chatty co-worker's life, whether you want to or not; and Sagittarius is happy to listen to all your news, but, be warned, this sign finds it hard to keep a secret. Finally, you get down to business: Sagittarius is a past master at displacement activities but these create thinking time.

This co-worker is a live wire, full of sparky ideas and good intentions. Many promises are made and Sagittarius is always happy to help out. Where Sagittarius falls down is on delivery. This sign is prone to take on far too much, and somehow no allowance is made for the time things take. Wise co-workers check schedules carefully. The creative side of Sagittarius comes out best in a free environment, so try to avoid too many rules.

Compatibility chart

Aries ★★★★★	Libra ★★★★★
Taurus ★★	Scorpio ★
Gemini ★★★★★	Sagittarius ★★★★★
Cancer ★	Capricorn ★
Leo ★★★★★	Aquarius ★★★★
Virgo ★★	Pisces ★

Capricorn

the goat

22 December – 19 January
Positive • Cardinal • Earth

Capricorn has the natural sensuality of an earth sign, but you also have the innate caution and sexual inhibitions bestowed by your ruler Saturn. This planet gifts you great resilience and strength of character but brings you face to face with duty. Saturn stands guard at the limit of conscious awareness maintaining the status quo, so this is the planet of marriage. The rigid boundaries of this stern planet can lead to separation between your powerful libido and your body. Cautious about expressing your carnal passion, you learn control and continence early in life and delay sexual gratification in favour of climbing the ladder of ambition. Yours is a serious sign and Capricorn is sober and responsible – while you are young. As you mature you become much lighter hearted, growing into your wisdom. Most Capricorns find that lecherous old age suits them rather well.

What makes you tick: cautiously moving into love

A passive, feminine, receptive sign, that is ruled by the bleakest, coldest, hardest and most masculine planet, it is no wonder Capricorn finds it hard to deal with emotional matters. There is a marked difference between male and female Capricorns. Men tend to identify with cold-hearted Saturn; women with the softer, feminine side of the sign. However, naturally there is cross-fertilization.

Valuing home and family, you adhere to strict rules and sexual mores, and are somewhat uptight about sex. There is a strong carnal appetite in earth signs and Capricorn has the added impetus of being an assertive cardinal sign, which can lead to a very horny goat. This sexy side usually comes out within the context of a committed relationship.

Your style
Committed, serious, attentive, utterly reliable and highly ambitious.

The female Capricorn is more in touch with her earthy sensual nature, and her need to feel safe and secure in a relationship. You are more able to show your feelings but may opt for the apparent security of marriage to an older man, a 'sugar daddy' who fulfils your material rather than emotional needs.

It is the influence of repressive Saturn that creates your emotional inhibitions. Fortunately for you Capricorn is a sign that paradoxically becomes younger and more light-hearted the older you get: in the second half of life, you get the hang of relationships and emotional interchange. The positive side of Saturn means that you cannot be swayed by spurious arguments or sob-stories.

Capricorn is fond of the words 'should' and 'ought'. You can give yourself a hard time trying to live up to the standards you set for yourself and the expectations society has of you. Loosening up and practising the art of 'live and let live' can be beneficial.

Your relationship style

Given the right partner, your earthy sexuality comes to the fore and you throw off your inhibitions, although you find it somewhat difficult to express yourself emotionally. It is not that you do not have an affectionate nature, you do, but physical expression of how you are feeling comes under the scrutiny of judgemental Saturn.

Your seduction technique

Capricorn is serious about most things and satisfying your sex drive is no exception; but at heart you are looking for the security of a lasting relationship and tend to equate lust with love. When you set out to seduce, you show your steely charm but fear of failure may hold you back. Your sexual target may feel that he or she is being assessed for suitability rather than being seduced. It is only when you get to bed that the lecherous goat emerges.

Capricorn says
'Are you serious?'

What you seek
Security, regular sex, commitment, loyalty and marriage.

What turns you on

The knee is the erogenous zone for Capricorn and having the back of your knee stroked can be a great turn-on for you. But your whole skin is erogenous and sensuous massage creates enormous pleasure for you. You like the feel of fur against your skin and being stroked for hours in front of the fire helps you to find the feeling of security that urges you on to completion.

You and your fantasy

Capricorn sexual fantasy is earthy and erotic. Much of it takes place in your introspective self, although you are unlikely to admit to this as you value your privacy too much. However, you have an active fantasy life that is only peripherally to do with sex. You fantasize finding exactly the right partner, and you imagine how it would be to be fully successful in your life. That success, naturally, includes a partner. By way of a change, you may well fantasize about being swept off your feet by ungovernable passion.

How you behave as a partner

Capricorn is not comfortable with public shows of affection so your behaviour around a partner is somewhat formal. You do not go in for hand holding or smoochy moments unless you are in the privacy of your own home. Spontaneous gestures are not for you and you are more likely to buy someone a present to show how fond you are of them than to tell them so. Ambitious and hard-working, you put business before pleasure. It is important to you to keep your status-symbol home well supplied with material goods and, when you do buy gifts for your partner, they are practical and of good quality. You are capable of romantic gestures such as presenting a diamond ring as you dine *à deux* in an expensive restaurant, accompanied by an excellent bottle of wine. Initially cautious and mistrustful of a lover, once committed you want to spend all your time with your partner and do a great deal to ensure that the relationship runs smoothly. However, as a Capricorn you have control issues that you cannot put aside. You want to be the one in charge, you need to be looked up to in the relationship, to be master (or mistress) in your house and to be obeyed. You are not likely to enjoy a totally equal partnership and a wise partner allows you to have the illusion, if not the reality, of being head of the household.

Trust and intimacy
Closed, mistrustful.

Secret sexual desire
Domination.

What you expect from a partner

Loyalty, fidelity, conformity and obedience come high on Capricorn's list of requirements from a partner. You want someone who looks well groomed and who never lets you down in public. In private, it is a different matter. You want a considerate lover who gently unfurls your formidable sexuality, someone who can make you behave like the horny goat you were born to be.

When it ends

Gloom pervades your life when a relationship ends and you do all you can to string the connection out, even if you are the one to leave. You believe you have failed and Capricorn doesn't like to admit to mistakes. If you left you feel extremely responsible and make sure that those left behind are provided for. If you are the one who was left, you want your material security covered in the divorce.

Capricorn relationships

Understanding your Capricorn man

Your Capricorn man is addicted to structure and control: he wants his life to be well ordered and secure. Without these anchors he feels scarily vulnerable and, with stern taskmaster Saturn wagging an admonitory finger, he desperately seeks to regain his authority. Not that you would know from looking at him that he feels insecure: outwardly he is as confident as ever, which doesn't help in your personal relationship and you have gently to encourage him to unburden his soul. This is not a man who finds introspection easy, so he doesn't always know how he is feeling; and he is, in any case, uncomfortable with raw emotion. Inhibited about expressing what is to him something very personal, with trust and gentle encouragement he can learn the art of intimacy.

A Capricorn man constantly seeks approval from the outside world. He needs the big house, the executive car and the trophy wife to feel that he has made it and yet he is at his most comfortable within the close family unit. This is a man who takes his responsibilities very seriously indeed.

You need to understand something about the nature of Capricorn's ruler, Saturn, to understand fully your Capricorn man. Saturn is the Lord of Karma, and Capricorn buys into the belief that what goes round comes round. Saturn also represents wisdom and inner discipline which develop in middle age, usually out of saturnine adversity. This planet has an unhappy knack of

Capricorn man

Passion rating
★★★★

How to make it work
Remember that this man shows his feelings by actions not words and that he needs security at all times.

spreading doom and gloom, and a Capricorn man is prone to depression. Black moods descend suddenly and obliterate everything else. It is no good trying to jolly him along, it simply won't work. Give him a safe, contained space and it passes. Sometimes his black sense of humour helps: he sees the funny side of misfortune and can enjoy both slapstick and satire.

Understanding your Capricorn woman

A Capricorn woman is more introspective and likely to find the inner approval that takes her away from her constant need to be looked on with favour by the world. Exploring her strengths and accepting her weaknesses with less judgement than her male counterpart, she channels her sense of duty less rigidly and with more kindness to herself. That doesn't mean she feels any less accountable, however. A wise partner helps her to see that she cannot be responsible for policing the world. This is a woman with a strong urge towards spirituality. She needs something to believe in beyond the shackles of conventional religion, something which takes her to the highest part of her being.

Capricorn woman

Passion rating
★ ★ ★

How to make it work
Give her the security that she craves.

Other relationships

Capricorn friends are dependable, loyal and practical. While they have no time for emotional angst, they are incredibly well organized and can sort your life out in a trice. The advice you get here is down to earth and pragmatic. Your lover is causing you anguish? Leave! You need somewhere to live? Get yourself a mortgage – Capricorn places great faith in bricks and mortar and sees these symbols of worldly success. If you mention money worries, Capricorn soon has you sorted, and talked into a pension plan and insurance for everything you can think of along the way.

The only problem with your serious friend is that not as much attention is paid to friendship as is given to work, and you probably have to remind your friend that all work and no play makes Jack, or Jill, very dull indeed. As this is not a spontaneous person, it could be a good idea to organize something on a regular basis. This sign likes worthy activities, especially those geared towards the good of the community, but a trip to the mountains may be just what this goat needs. Getting out into the fresh air is always a tonic for this earth sign.

One thing that will surprise you about your Capricorn friend is the earthy, black sense of humour. While many Capricorns see life as full of gloom and responsibility, they are able to keep things in perspective by laughing at the ridiculousness of it all.

Capricorn is not a sign that is content with being a co-worker: this ambitious, highly organized and efficient sign feels much happier being in charge. So remember that your Capricorn co-worker is looking for boosts to his or her authority and will not tolerate being undermined in any way. This is a person who demands respect and who works best in a situation of mutual trust.

Your Capricorn co-worker quite naturally gravitates to a position of power, chairing meetings and so on. If you are able to tolerate this, then the relationship runs smoothly and a great deal is achieved. Hard-working Capricorn never slacks on the job and expects everyone else to show the same dedication to duty. This sign cannot tolerate incompetence of any kind. It may be necessary from time to time to remind your Capricorn co-worker to lighten up and enjoy life.

Compatibility chart

Aries ★ ★ ★ ★

Taurus ★ ★ ★ ★ ★

Gemini ★

Cancer ★ ★ ★ ★ ★

Leo ★

Virgo ★ ★ ★ ★

Libra ★ ★ ★ ★

Scorpio ★ ★

Sagittarius ★

Capricorn ★ ★ ★ ★ ★

Aquarius ★

Pisces ★ ★

Aquarius

the water carrier

20 January – 19 February

Positive • Fixed • Air

Rational Aquarius is traditionally the least emotional sign, but nevertheless has strong passions – although he or she finds it difficult to connect to them. You intellectualize, discuss and are motivated by lust and emotion, and enjoy experimenting with sex, but actually feeling the feelings perplexes you. You ask yourself: 'What is this thing called love?' Free-spirited, valuing your independence and individuality, and finding intimacy challenging, you nevertheless yearn for a settled relationship. When you find one you either stick with it no matter how bad, or you suddenly leave for no good reason; which means that, as a partner, you are something of an enigma. A sociable and outgoing sign, you need personal space and you have to do things differently. Always fair-minded you give equal value to the uniqueness of your partner.

What makes you tick: dispassionately falling into love

Perverse and unpredictable, Aquarius is a sign that simply has to be *different*. On principle you never do what you are expected to do, which is the influence of your ruler Uranus, and yet you can get stuck in the most eccentric rut, influenced by your co-ruler Saturn. These two planets battle it out in your psyche and, when an irresistible force meets an immovable object, chaos can result. A wise Aquarius channels these energies into transformation rather than head-on confrontation, and many become analysts, scientists or therapists.

As an Aquarius you probably feel that you don't actually belong on this planet. You get on with humanity as a whole much better than in one-to-one situations but you can sometimes feel like a scientist peering at an experiment, trying to understand what makes humanity tick. This is because you are cut off from your feelings. Your symbol, the water carrier, bears emotions neatly enclosed in the water pot and that is the way you like them, anything else is inconvenient. You intensely dislike emotional messiness, encouraging others to follow your example and rise above them into rational objectivity. Your conundrum is to uncork the emotions within yourself.

Your style

Dispassionate, formal, self-contained and a workaholic.

You find it incredibly difficult to express your feelings about anything personal or intimate, although you are extremely articulate about where humanity is going and what it is doing to itself. Your social conscience and concern for humanity drive you forwards, you want to bring rebellion and revolution to overturn the status quo, and you have a deep desire to improve the future. Many Aquarians live in the brave new world of possibilities, coming into the present moment is a challenge you do not relish.

Your relationship style

You have difficulty with intimacy and yet you belong to a fixed sign that, secretly, wants stability. So finding the right partner is a great relief to you, although you still take things step by step and wait for your partner to commit first. Up until that time you hold yourself aloof, finding an outlet for your sexual urges without getting involved, so you have flings. When you do find a partner, outside the bedroom you are coolly affectionate although you may surprise your partner with a romantic gesture or two or with some wild sex in a very unexpected place.

With Uranus as your ruler, whatever the next sexual trend is going to be, you have already been there so you need a partner who is prepared to experiment both sexually and with different types of relationships, and you may play out your freedom—commitment dilemma through free love, although you may chose celibacy just to be different.

> **Aquarius says**
> 'Have you tried ... ?'
>
> **What you seek**
> Casual sex, mental stimulation, companionship; possibly marriage, certainly something unconventional.

Your seduction technique

Whatever Aquarius does is a little different: your aloof sexual style is one of contrariness and contrast. You have quite a strong sex drive, and positively crackle with electricity. This can be exciting for potential lovers, and yet there is little connection to your dispassionate head so you don't act on the signals your body, or a prospective lover, sends you; and if you do it may be over in a flash. Then, on the other hand, you can be romantic and sweetly seductive using candles to enhance your allure.

What turns you on

Strictly speaking your erogenous zones are the calves and ankles but you may receive little pleasure from your lover stroking these areas, especially if the touch is somewhat heavy. Aquarius prefers things to be light and airy, and wants to be stimulated intellectually. You usually finds what goes on in your own head a much greater turn-on than anything your partner may do.

You and your fantasy

Aquarius is a great sign for fantasy, the more inventive and bizarre the better, and many Aquarius fantasies involve outer space and alien abduction. You rarely repeat a fantasy twice although you may have a favourite that you will come back to. The sex is kinky and there is every chance you want to act this fantasy out with your partner, given the right setting.

How you behave as a partner

As you tend not to be bound by conventions, and hate to be bored, you are likely to have an unconventional setup. You need space and freedom and if a partner demands fidelity, you instantly look for the next relationship. Not that you necessarily leave your partner, but you make the point that you cannot be tied down. On the other hand you can be an extremely loyal and faithful lover.

Intellectual companionship is vital for you and you want a partner who can share your interest in what makes humanity tick, and who is prepared to do something positive about the state of the world.

Rather than intimacy you want a meeting of minds. You are very concerned with your partner's personal growth and do all you can to encourage further study and exploration. You enjoy rationally discussing progress and are extremely supportive if issues come up that you can assist with objectively. You have the knack of helping someone rise up out of the mire into the light of a new awareness.

Trust and intimacy

Detached and dispassionate.

Secret sexual desire

Emotional meltdown.

What you expect from a partner

You would rather like your partner to be around when you want company, and elsewhere the remainder of the time. Your personal space is very important to you and you may prefer to occupy separate houses. A partner who has plenty of outside interests and a supportive group of friends is ideal, particularly as you refuse to get involved in your partner's emotional angst. You probably won't mind the odd lover or two, there is not a jealous bone in your body, so Aquarians have some rather strange arrangements by other signs' standards. What you do not forgive is a partner who tries to take away your freedom.

When it ends

Endings are difficult for your contradictory sign. You are very fixed and yet your co-ruler is unpredictable Uranus who is prone to throwing the baby out with the bathwater. You could up and leave everything, or hold on at all costs. In many ways it is easier for you if your partner leaves, at least you know where you stand.

Aquarius relationships

Understanding your Aquarius man

This is a very complex man indeed, and an unpredictable one, and what you see is definitely not all there is. Your Aquarius man appears to be insensitive because of his emotional disconnection but he is acutely sensitive to subtle nuances of mood and behaviour, and he uses his intuitive knowledge to protect himself against the ravages of other people's emotions. He finds it extremely difficult to open up and tell you how he feels, so you have to intuit this for yourself.

This man has a problem. He desperately wants to maintain his individuality, and pushes you away or does exactly the opposite of what you wish simply to make the point that he stands alone. And yet somewhere in the depths of his being he is seeking a soul mate who anchors him to the planet and makes him feel he has come home. Of course he never tells you this, or if he does (because you can never predict exactly what Aquarius will do) he argues the case for soul mates with cynical and dispassionate rationality. But secretly, in the depths of his

Aquarius man

Passion rating
★ ★ ★

How to make it work
Give him time and space; remember intimacy and commitment are alien territory for him.

romantic heart, he really does believe there is someone out there, a one-off, one and only, twin soul. It is unlikely that you are this paragon, but the idea of it is enough to hold him to you until he falls in love with your finer qualities.

The conflict between his two rulers, Uranus and Saturn, cannot be overstated. The two opposite extremes of the zodiac are trying to find space in one psyche. In all areas of his life he faces a dilemma: should he live within the limits set by Saturn, or bring in the transformation that revolutionary Uranus is urging? In an effort to resolve the conflict, he is often meticulous as a way to be in control, or wildly eccentric and totally out of control. The problem for you is that one can easily masquerade as the other.

Understanding your Aquarius woman

An Aquarius woman can be somewhat easier to understand than her male counterpart as she is more aware of emotions, but she nevertheless remains tantalizingly out of reach. Making an emotional connection to her is problematic, becoming intimate even more so. She is likely to do, or say, the most bizarre things and wise partners learn how to let it ride; she is not being personal. Abrupt, tactless and unconventional, she did not mean to insult you, that is just the way it came out. But she is a sensitive soul underneath who needs to feel loved and who, once she has committed to you, is loyal for life.

Aquarius woman

Passion rating
★ ★ ★

How to make it work
Cherish her difference; remember she comes from another planet.

Other relationships

Aquarius friends are much easier to connect with than Aquarius lovers because the fear of emotional intimacy has been removed and they feel no pressure to maintain their separateness when with you. This is a sociable and gregarious sign who enjoys being part of a crowd. Or rather, enjoys people-watching and that happens best in a crowd although your friend may stand slightly aloof. A person born under this sign is a shrewd observer of human nature.

This is the friend to take on a shopping trip for the future. Aquarius has a great eye for innovative design or the latest technology and is an excellent adviser – and a patient teacher; this is someone who enjoys sharing knowledge.

Your Aquarius friend is also a staunch ally in a crisis, but don't expect sympathy. After a peremptory 'Sorry about that' your friend helps you move out of your misery and into an objective assessment of the situation. With this shrewd mind at work it won't be long before your problem is solved. Your heart might be broken, in which case you'll have to go elsewhere for TLC, but your personal life is sorted.

And if you want to do something different, this is the friend to talk to. Aquarians positively celebrate the uniqueness of everyone.

As a co-worker Aquarius is also something of a contradiction – an interesting combination of the shrewd with the intuitive, the rational with the leap of faith. He or she is friendly enough and keenly absorbed in the work provided it is intellectually challenging or socially rewarding, and your Aquarius co-worker often works well as part of a team, but, and it is a big but, this individualistic sign also wants to do things their way. It can be useful to listen to Aquarius' suggestions: this innovative mind is keenly attuned to the next new thing, the trend that will hit in a year or two's time, the invention that will save the planet and so on. Give your Aquarius co-worker his or her creative head and an Aquarius in the business could be excellent news.

Compatibility chart

Aries ★★★★★	Libra ★★★★
Taurus ★★★	Scorpio ★★★
Gemini ★★★★	Sagittarius ★★★
Cancer ★★★	Capricorn ★
Leo ★★★★★	Aquarius ★★★★★
Virgo ★★★	Pisces ★

Pisces
the fishes

20 February – 20 March
Passive • Mutable • Water

E veryday reality is too harsh for you – Pisces is an incurable romantic. So enamoured are you with love that you confuse lust, infatuation, and gentle affection for the real thing. You believe that sex equals love; the two are joined like the fishes in your glyph. You want to merge totally into your lover; for you there can be no barriers between you. Fluid and ever-changing, you become whatever your lover wants you to be. You can be so enmeshed you do not know where you end and your lover begins. Your past partners have a pull on your heart strings and you may have sex out of pity. With your watery sensitivity you instinctively know what your partner is feeling and can respond to unspoken desires.

What makes you tick: escaping into love

Pisces is a deeply emotional and complex sign: beneath the surface you are pulled this way and that by subconscious currents and desires over which you have no control. This makes it difficult for you to understand yourself and almost impossible for other signs to do so. You see parts of yourself reflected back through other people's eyes but find it hard to separate what is really you from what is them, especially as you intuitively feel what is going on inside them but cannot make rational sense of it.

Deeply empathic and compassionate, you have a strong desire to save the world, or a person – which is bad news for your relationships. When in saviour or rescuer mode, you have no discrimination: you give and give, and then find that you have flipped into victim or martyr. If you find yourself saying: 'What did I do to deserve this?' or 'After all I've done for you ...' you are back in that old role. This is especially so in relationships and many Pisces are deeply disappointed to find that the perfect love they thought they had found is but another chapter in the old scenario. However, your forgiving nature rarely learns from this and you are taken advantage of over and over again.

Often the world is too harsh for your sensitive nature and you long for escape. The escape route can be through another person, a fantasy or a bottle. Yours is one of the most addicted signs of the zodiac, although the addiction does not have to be to a substance. You are addicted to romance and sometimes unwittingly invite emotional abuse by your naive trust. You simply cannot believe that anything bad could happen again, and yet your need for love and romance never waivers.

Your style
Emotional, intimate, intermittent, helpful and involved.

Your relationship style

Your relationship style is romantic and impractical. When it works it is blissful but you have an unhappy knack of becoming a victim to love. Yearning for a close relationship, you lose yourself in your partner. You choose a partner because that person needs you rather than because you are truly in love and you often find yourself supporting your partner out of pity. As a result you stay in relationships long after it would have been sensible to leave.

Your seduction technique

A romantic at heart, you enjoy the whole business of fishing for a partner, although you flirt outrageously and could well merely be keeping your hand in. No one, even you, can tell the difference. You mesmerize potential partners, drawing them in with your beddable eyes and promising them the world. However, little do they know that this is a promise that could well be gone by morning.

Pisces says
'I've found another soul mate.'

What you seek
Love, romance, emotional melding, marriage.

What turns you on

Pisces is in love with being in love and for you a prospective lover is the greatest turn-on. Your emotions are probably your biggest erogenous zone but your feet are pretty erotic too. Having them stroked, and sucking or nibbling at your toes sends you into transports of delight.

You and your fantasy

You live in the inner world of your imagination and your daydreams have substance for you. You fantasize about finding your one and only true soul mate, the perfect love affair and saving the world. These three often merge together and many of your fantasies are out of this world. You step into myth and magic to find your fantasy partner and the problem lies in ascertaining which of your lovers is imaginary and which is real. Not that it matters to you: you prefer to see the world through rose-coloured glasses.

How you behave as a partner

Pisces is a loyal, although not necessary faithful, partner. Professing fidelity, in reality you have no problem carrying on two relationships at once. You desperately care about your partner, to such an extent that you may swallow them up, and you cannot conceive of being parted. The emotional ties bind you close; or at least they bind one part of you. There are two sides to your nature operating in tandem – one consciously, the other unconsciously. The unconscious part does the opposite of the conscious. So, while you are swearing undying love, another part of you is casting around for another lover and you rarely end one relationship before another begins. Pisces enjoys having a secret lover, or more than one lover, lurking in the shadows. Yours is a faithless sign.

You flirt and suss out potential new partners, and may even swim off altogether for a while, but you will be back albeit to play the martyr. This is something that your partner quickly learns. Like those two fishes in your glyph that are swimming in opposite directions but remain tied together, you may leave emotionally but remain physically present, or you may leave physically and remain emotionally present. You have no intention of hurting your partner, but you cannot help yourself.

You do not tell your partner what you need, nor do you voice your disappointment when the relationship fails to live up to its romantic promise. For you the relationship is all.

Trust and intimacy
Naive, promiscuously intimate.

Secret sexual desire
Utterly selfish sex.

What you expect from a partner

You see your partner as an extension of yourself. Because you have merged with him or her, you expect your partner instinctively to know how you feel and what you need. You don't want to be asked how you feel, you can't put it into words, but you do want your partner to show a constant interest in how you are. You have a deep hunger for empathy and compassion, and yearn for the consideration you show your partner to be reflected back to you through your partner's actions.

When it ends

There is a big problem here. Pisces doesn't actually end things! You may leave, sometimes for years, but the legal niceties are overlooked because somehow that would be too final, and anyway the emotional connection has never been broken. You still feel something for your partner, even if you are living with someone else. Then you may come swimming back, or not. It is all the same to elusive Pisces.

Pisces relationships

Understanding your Pisces man

Just when you think you've achieved the impossible and understood this complex and lyrical lover, he swims off in another direction and you realize you don't know him at all. Like a chameleon he effortlessly blends in to his surroundings and becomes whatever you want him to be. Little that your Pisces man does stems from rational thought. He reacts constantly to the subtle emotional stimuli he receives through his psychic antennae, intertwined with his own emotional desires. If he can't understand himself, how can you expect to keep track of this fluid character?

This man has a soft heart and is easily taken in. A dual sign, he has two natures that swim in opposite directions: whatever appears on the surface, something very different is going on out of sight. This confuses your man as much as you. He doesn't intend to spin webs of illusion and deceit, but he does. And then he suffers agonies of guilt: he didn't intend to hurt you, and he wants to atone. The hint of burning flesh is strong around a Pisces. With his powerful escapist fantasies, he inhabits a different world. His world is sensitive, empathic, emotional and, despite outward appearances, totally self-absorbed. While one part of him continually thinks of others, the other part is trying to get his needs met.

Pisces man

Passion rating

★★★

How to make it work

Remember you are the living embodiment of his perfect dream, you have to handle reality.

As he never voices these needs, and is rarely consciously aware of what they are, he suffers when he is disappointed. He needs to be needed, and to be understood at an emotional level. For Pisces man intimacy is all about emotional melding, becoming one. For him one and one don't make two, they make a physical, emotional and spiritual union.

You need to understand how fluid his truth can be. Partly out of a desire not to hurt anyone, but perhaps more because of that dual nature, your Pisces man isn't really sure what truth is. Whatever it is he is economical with it and Pisces is adept at little white lies that just get bigger and bigger. It is hard to tell what is reality and what is fantasy with this imaginative man.

Understanding your Pisces woman

Your Pisces woman is sultry and lush, she cannot help turning on her sexual magnets whenever a potential suitor is near, no matter how committed to you she may feel. She swims in a river of deep emotions and intuitive impressions, and she doesn't always know how she feels. She needs you to reflect feelings back to her so that they can become more conscious. Her romantic dreams leave her even more vulnerable to love than her male counterpart. No matter how many disappointments she has had, naively trusting, she still has high hopes of her relationship with you. Her desire to be united makes her vulnerable so do not take advantage of her.

Pisces woman

Passion rating
★ ★ ✦

How to make it work
Accept that you will never pin her down.

Other relationships

Pisces is an exceptionally sympathetic friend, and this is exactly the right companion for a tear-jerker movie – most Pisces love the sentimental nostalgia of old black-and-white films. You can cry together, emote together or wallow in self-pity if the mood takes you. Your Pisces friend knows exactly how you are feeling and follows your lead. Taking on the emotional colouring of whatever surrounds him or her, Pisces makes it pretty hard actually to get to know what is going on behind those big eyes. You sometimes get the feeling that it is all an act, but that may simply be because your friend finds it hard to separate reality from fantasy. While your Pisces friend is wonderfully understanding, in a crisis, a tendency to wallow in it with you is not the most constructive help a friend could offer you. But if you need to make a confession, or seek absolution, this is the place to go. If you have relationship troubles, you receive a sympathetic hearing but Pisces' desire to maintain a relationship at all costs might colour the advice you are given.

What your Pisces friend never willingly does is hurt you, although a tendency to disappear at crucial moments could well lead to a certain lack of trust between you. Your friend may not have noticed that months can elapse between your meetings, and when he or she returns Pisces focuses full attention on you once more. This is a sign that lives from moment to moment and expects you to be waiting for that return.

To understand your Pisces co-worker properly, you need to grasp how much of a sacrifice he or she is prepared to make on your behalf: this person gives their all, and then some. Your co-worker offers you compassion, understanding, sympathy, help, assistance, love and romance – all prettily packaged in a box marked 'guilt trip' if you don't express your undying appreciation. This is the problem: with an innate tendency to martyrdom, nature compels your Pisces co-worker to make a burnt offering of him- or herself, regardless of your wishes in the matter. Pisces will promise you the world, but you rely on this co-worker at your peril. Just when needed most, Pisces swims off.

Compatibility chart

Aries ★

Taurus ★ ★ ★ ★

Gemini ★ ★

Cancer ★ ★ ★ ★ ★

Leo ★ ★ ★

Virgo ★ ★ ★ ★ ★

Libra ★ ★ ★ ★

Scorpio ★ ★ ★ ★

Sagittarius ★

Capricorn ★

Aquarius ★

Pisces ★ ★ ★ ★ ★

Part 2

ELEMENTAL ATTRACTION

The zodiac wheel is criss-crossed with subtle energy flows that attract or repel. Each sun sign belongs to one of four elements and the energies of these elements interact with each other in specific ways, some harmonious, others not. A fundamental part of human sexual attraction, the elements are important in all relationships. People who share the same element get along well together and make empathic friends and colleagues, as well as lovers. People from disparate elements approach life from different perspectives, which can create unintentional misunderstandings. Notwithstanding, opposites attract and exciting partnerships, and stimulating friendships, occur between opposite, but compatible, elements on the zodiac wheel.

Planets also influence attraction. The passionate pair Venus and Mars are fundamental to understanding yourself and your partner as they can powerfully affect and modify basic sun-sign urges. If your libido doesn't run true to your sun sign, the explanation lies with virile Mars or voluptuous Venus. The potent duo have a turbulent relationship and are powerful attractors – or repellers – across charts, pulling the most unlikely couples together or thrusting apart the most compatible of sun signs.

Elemental affinities

The four astrological elements are fire, earth, air and water. They represent different ways of perceiving and interacting with the world, and people whose sun signs are in the same element approach life in the same way and feel at ease with one another. However, some people have a very strong emphasis on a particular element in their birthchart, because a large number of planets in their chart are placed in signs that share that element, and this can make them behave rather differently to their sun-sign element. (You can check this or the position of Venus and Mars on a properly calculated birthchart.)

Fire, the element of the spirit, is creative and intuitive, and this outgoing element needs people with whom to be active. Earth, the physical element, is pragmatic and sense-oriented. This self-sufficient element has its feet firmly on the ground. Air, the intellectual element, is communicative and mind-oriented, wanting other people to bounce ideas off. Water, the emotional element, is empathic and feeling-oriented, needing people with whom to share emotions.

Each element has its own agenda. Fire is looking for stimulation but craves freedom. This is the element of hot sex, one-night stands, dates that lead nowhere, and marriage is a major challenge. Earth is looking for security and seeks permanence. This is the element of long, slow courtship and enduring marriage. Flirtatious air is looking for mental understanding, and seeks an intellectually stimulating companion with whom to share ideas. Water is looking for a deep emotional connection, and the greater part of a water-sign relationship takes place in the imagination. Water seeks a lasting partnership.

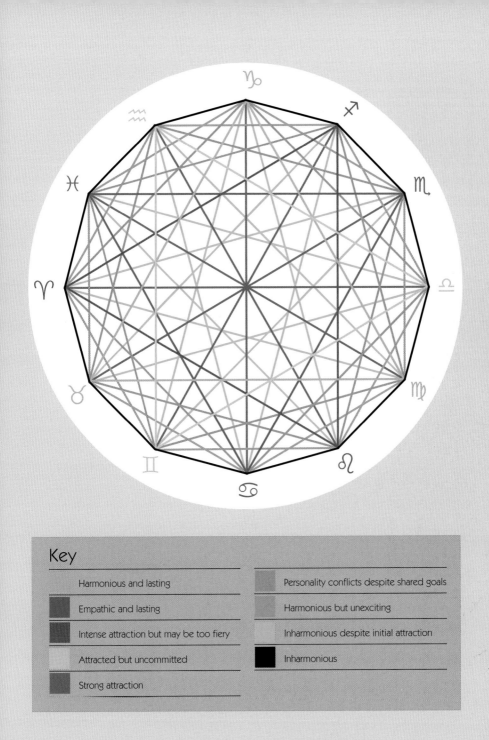

Key

	Harmonious and lasting		Personality conflicts despite shared goals
	Empathic and lasting		Harmonious but unexciting
	Intense attraction but may be too fiery		Inharmonious despite initial attraction
	Attracted but uncommitted		Inharmonious
	Strong attraction		

Fire

Aries • Leo • Sagittarius

Outgoing fire people have an enormous appetite for life, love, raw sex and unabashed lust. You want an uncomplicated sex life and rarely confuse lust with love. Capable of great passion, you fall headlong into lust, and out again as quickly. This inspired element seeks new experiences and has no time for subtle seduction. Adventurous fire people try anything at least once and act out their fantasies with enthusiasm.

Lovers

Fire signs are the sexual gymnasts of the zodiac. Fiery people go all out for what you want and are upfront about your sexual desires, having difficulty delaying gratification for a moment longer than is absolutely necessary. Less blatant signs find fire people brash and immodest, but may still get swept up in the conflagration. Freedom-loving fire is rarely to be denied.

Fire people are hard to pin down and take time to make a commitment that is lasting, although fleeting lusts are common – and all-consuming while they last. Fire people have no difficulty in saying 'I love you', the difficulty comes in staying around to prove it. Too much intensity, or a hint of possessiveness, and you take off, so wise lovers play hard to get and let you make the running. You want to conquer, but enjoy the thrill of the chase almost as much as the finale.

When you get it on, the sex is hot. Foreplay is an art until you become too impatient to wait. Creative fire people have an active imagination and few inhibitions, enjoying indulging sexual fantasies to the full.

Sexual style
Tempestuous, lustful, uncomplicated.

Seduction tools
Flattery and a good time.

Erogenous zone
The sense of humour.

Other relationships

Fun-loving fire people make excellent friends and are never dull. Relishing theatre, music and bars, you spend many happy hours socializing. Or flirting. Fire people believe in keeping in practice, married or not, and many fire friends are bed-buddies because it's a companionable thing to do and doesn't imply commitment. But people should not expect to be your only 'best friend', there will be a multitude! As with fiery lovers any hint of possessiveness sends you racing for space. You will never be tied down, but you accord everyone the same freedom.

You enjoy surprising people and are always ready to party. But if you see someone you fancy you'll pursue. Wise friends fade uncomplainingly into the background, or seek their own adventures. When you return the adventure is raked over with great delight. If friends are having problems, you are sympathetic and won't hesitate to offer advice on how to get out of trouble. It won't all be practical, but it could change their life.

Whirlwind activity, lots of energy, and creative spontaneity accompany a fiery co-worker but chaos can ensue, as can fierce competitiveness. You are an innovator, but hate routine and follow-up, preferring to delegate. You say 'Why don't we ...' just when the plan is complete. The trouble is you are often right, although ideas may be impractical or expensive. One thing is certain: working life is never dull with you around.

Approach to life
Expansive, creative, full-on, active and spontaneous.

Wants
Raw sex and great adventures.

Says
'Let's do it!'

Earth

Taurus • Virgo • Capricorn

Earth is the most pragmatic and practical element, and while self-contained on the surface, earth people enjoy pandering to their bodies. You interact with the world through your senses: touch, taste and smell being vital to you. Food is an important part of your sexual or friendship rituals. Earth people thrive on routine and dislike surprises, but there is nothing you like more than the certainty of good friends.

Lovers

Your down-to-earth, lusty element is pragmatic about sex, recognizing it as a basic human need that requires regular satisfaction. Earth people invented extended foreplay and you happily spend hours massaging or stroking a partner, provided the surroundings are comfortable – comfort is important to you and discomfort is a great turn-off. With a strong, but well-controlled, sex drive, you willingly delay ultimate gratification in pursuit of sensual pleasure but, sadly, love of routine may lead to a somewhat boring sex life, and some signs find your lack of emotional connection disconcerting. Wise partners gently encourage earth lovers to try something new, and your appetite can be aroused by sensory experiences.

Seduction tools
Good food, sensual oils for massage and a comfortable bed.

Erogenous zone
The skin and physical senses.

You are cautious but extremely loyal, preferring to get to know prospective partners slowly, usually over several excellent meals. With such a strong need for security, you have an eye to marriage and prospective partners should not be surprised to find themselves discussing financial assets as well as sexual ones. Married partners can look forward to growing old together in comfort but should bear in mind that you find it somewhat difficult to say 'I love you.'

Other relationships

Earth people make good and dependable, if at times predictable, friends. You happily meet every Friday night for 10 or 20 years, and look forward to holidaying in the same place as last year, and the year before that. You go in for lifelong 'best friends', preferring a few really good friends to a horde of acquaintances. With your love of good food and wine, you make excellent hosts, and can be witty and entertaining companions.

Earth friends are the ones people turn to for good advice. You are extremely supportive in a crisis, provided you understand what is going on: emotional or existential angst is not your forte but give you something practical to do and you excel. You are the friend to call when water gushes through the ceiling or someone is locked out at two in the morning. You won't let anyone down.

Your reliability and solid common sense make you an excellent co-worker, especially for more flighty signs. You are never late, or miss a deadline or mislay important papers. You have the information to hand and know exactly how far a plan has progressed. There are times when more adaptable co-workers could scream with frustration when you insist on following the routine; but at other times, they are thankful that you did.

Approach to life

Physical, sensory, pragmatic, cautious.

Wants

Plenty of foreplay, carnal sex, and certainty.

Says

'That was sensational!'

Air

Gemini • Libra • Aquarius

Air is the mental element and you live in your head, or on the net. Exploring an exciting world of ideas, you communicate what you find: discussion is your staple diet. Other people are important as sounding boards and you find it difficult to be out of contact, but you are capable of ignoring the needs of your body for long periods. It is not so much a question of delaying gratification as of not even noticing desire exists. For you truth is what is happening at that moment and what is happening in your head is more exciting than the feeling in your body as, for you, love is a cerebral activity.

Lovers

Air people enjoy a wide variety of relationships and you find it difficult to be exclusively committed to one person. Flirtatious conversation is as important as breathing, and phone sex suits you just fine. You can appear fickle and superficial. 'Love you' is said freely, accompanied by air kisses to all and sundry. Elements who need an attentive mate find air lovers difficult, but if they can relax and enjoy your sociability, there is every chance that you will go home together. If all else fails you can always try telephone sex or a chat room.

Seduction tools
Words, ideas and companionship.

Erogenous zone
Between the ears.

Many air people dislike being touched and get off on a mind meld. Your libido may be low but you can be talked into bed, and one of the most effective ways to seduce you is to let you talk yourself into it. Once involved your inventive mind finds plenty to explore and, as mental rapport is more important than sexual attraction, wise signs keep you talking.

Other relationships

Sociable air signs make excellent companions but even a casual acquaintance is a best friend – for the moment. You love to gossip and bitch, and sit around a coffee pot for hours, although at the same time you are on the phone to at least three people and waving to a dozen more. If others are not present, you talk about them. If someone wants your total attention, they need to put you in a soundproof box. Once there you listen avidly, and then spill the news to the world. No one should expect you to keep their secrets, it is an impossibility. Nor should they rely on you too heavily; when they need you most, something else catches your attention. But if they need to know something, it is always worth phoning you. If you don't know, you know someone who does.

You are an ideas person and are excellent in situations that require communication and innovation. Where you are less effective as co-workers is where you have to follow routine. Air people hate dull jobs and quietly unload them. You need to structure the day to avoid boredom setting in – you become lethal with nothing to do. If you are stimulated you are happy. And a happy air person moves things along nicely.

Approach to life
Cerebral, communicative, playful and inquisitive.

Wants
Mental rapport and pillow talk.

Says
'Let's talk about it!'

Water

Cancer • Scorpio • Pisces

Water is the most emotional element and water people are passive and romantic despite their powerful instinctual needs. Highly sensitive and attuned to delicate nuances of feeling, yours is the duplicitous element of covert persuasion and subtle seduction. You see what other people want, and offer it to them as a way of feeling needed. You have your own inner rhythm, and much of your behaviour stems from feelings arising at each moment.

You crave contact with people, satisfaction comes through emotional rather than sexual sharing, and you long for blissful submersion in another person, although sex is sometimes torrid. Your empathic element makes other people feel loved and understood by reflecting back their subtle and often unnoticed emotions.

Lovers

Water is the seductive and sentimental element in the zodiac and Water people confuse desire with love. Needing to be needed you are an empathic lover inclined to lose yourself in your partner, sharing and experiencing yourself through a deep exchange of feelings. If love is not forthcoming, you settle for lust but convince yourself that it is forever. If all else fails you resort to fantasy and illusion. Water boundaries are permeable and other elements feel that they are being engulfed as you cannot understand their need to maintain individuality. Your vulnerable watery feelings can be terribly hurt by the insensitivity of more robust signs.

You can be very romantic, especially as part of your subtle seduction technique. Yours is the hearts and flowers element that really wants to make a relationship last, and finds it impossible to let go.

Seduction tools
Emotional manipulation, candles, music.

Erogenous zone
The emotions.

Other relationships

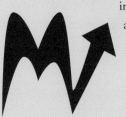

Water friends are the ones people go to for sympathy and comfort. You cry with your friends and share their pain as well as their joy. You make someone feel they are the only person in the world whose company is desired – but this is a fallacy people would do well not to rely on. With your soft heart you may be so taken up with caring for others that friendship has to wait. You have a tendency to swim off, sometimes for months or even years at a time, and then float back into friends' lives as though you never left. In your heart you have not been parted, the emotional connection was still there and so what if you forgot to write. They knew you loved them, didn't they?

Water people are intuitively aware of the feelings of people around them. You notice who is feeling down, you remember birthdays and ask after family and pets. You step in if someone is ill. But you are also the person who takes offence at an insensitive remark, or an imagined slight, and who can make 'poor me' into an art form. You need to be aware of just how much you need to be needed.

Approach to life

Emotional, soft-hearted, romantic, sensitive and gullible.

Wants

Subtle seduction and emotional merging.

Says

'This is how I feel.'

Elemental combinations

Fire and fire

PARTNERS A red-hot, lustful pairing but quickly ignited passion may burn out just as fast. This tempestuous relationship is never dull!

OTHER RELATIONSHIPS Despite being excellent friends and colleagues, fireworks erupt as both parties passionately defend their views. Fortunately, fire signs do not hold grudges and arguments are over as quickly as they blew up.

Fire and earth

PARTNERS Carnal desire creates a lusty partnership, unless pragmatic earth puts out the flames. But, beware, fire signs hate routine and boredom may set in.

OTHER RELATIONSHIPS An interesting balancing act. Earth is fired up by fire, and fire is calmed by earth. Fire leads, earth follows – and gets stuck with the routine tasks. Can it last? Earth has to adapt to fire or lose out.

Fire and air

PARTNERS You feed each other. With flames fanned by air, passion ignites quickly and torrid sex ensues, but may burn out equally fast. Long-term commitment is difficult.

OTHER RELATIONSHIPS A talkative and active pairing; lasting friendships full of fun and adventure. Creative ideas abound, but routine tasks are ignored and chaos may ensue.

Fire and water

PARTNERS This produces scalding steam, or a damp squib. Water can be too emotional for freedom-loving fire, and water finds it hard to cope with fire's flirtatious ways.

OTHER RELATIONSHIPS A tricky combination in which hurt feelings abound. Fire gets impatient with water's sensitivity, and water feels trampled upon.

Earth and earth

PARTNERS A stable and lasting combination. This relationship is long, slow and sensual – if you ever get started that is.

OTHER RELATIONSHIPS You are totally loyal to each other, and very reliable, but may become bogged down in inertia and the mundane.

Air and air

PARTNERS Will you ever stop talking long enough to get down to it? The relationship is all mouth.

OTHER RELATIONSHIPS You know how to change the world, but won't get round to it. The energy is best employed in creative pursuits.

Earth and air

PARTNERS Air finds it hard to breathe under the weight of earth; earth gets exasperated at air's frivolity. This works best when earth provides the material resources and air arranges intellectual stimulation.

OTHER RELATIONSHIPS A useful pair: air supplies the ideas, and earth follows through.

Air and water

PARTNERS Will you ever understand each other? One emotes, the other thinks. The fantasy does not survive the reality.

OTHER RELATIONSHIPS Air spends hours explaining how it thinks, water tries to show how it feels, but the two just don't jell.

Earth and water

PARTNERS Very touchy feely. These two produce an enduring partnership, or a soggy mess.

OTHER RELATIONSHIPS These two usually manage to get along despite having little in common. Both are too placid to argue.

Water and water

PARTNERS There is lifelong empathy, emotions run deep and bind you together – even after parting.

OTHER RELATIONSHIPS You are sympathetic friends and nurturing colleagues.

Opposites attract

Polarity is the yin and yang of the zodiac. Signs have positive or negative energy and these complementary poles alternate round the zodiac wheel. 'Negative' attribution is to do with polarity not attitude. Introverted negative polarity, or feminine, signs are passive and receptive. Outgoing positive polarity, or masculine, signs are active and initiating. Both are needed for balance and neither is better than the other. Water and earth elements are negative; fire and air positive.

Signs opposite each other on the zodiac wheel attract because of shared polarity: these pairings feel comfortable because energy flows in the same direction. In extroverted positive signs the energy flow is outwards; and in introverted negative signs, it is inwards. Each sign in a polarity pairing can benefit from the other as each has complementary skills and abilities.

The active pairings of Aries–Libra, Gemini–Sagittarius, Leo–Aquarius attract because they share externally focused energies, and combine complementary air and fire elements. These initiating signs are easily roused, need little foreplay and don't wait to be asked. On the surface positive signs have stronger libido and appear to be more passionate, but they lack commitment and stamina.

The passive pairings of Taurus–Scorpio, Cancer–Capricorn, Virgo–Pisces attract because they share inwardly focused energies, and combine supportive earth and water elements. These signs are slower to rouse, enjoy prolonged foreplay and wait to be asked. While appearing passive deep down there is a strong sex drive and a desire to commit.

Unlike a magnet pairings between positive and negative signs repel unless other factors intervene, as inharmonious elements have a totally different approach to life. Where an active and a passive sign do get together there is a potential for complementing each other's style, but one may well suck energy from the other leaving the normally ebullient positive sign exhausted, or the usually passive receptive sign over-energized. Opposite signs share another zodiac quality: they are cardinal, fixed or mutable. Energetic and ambitious cardinal signs

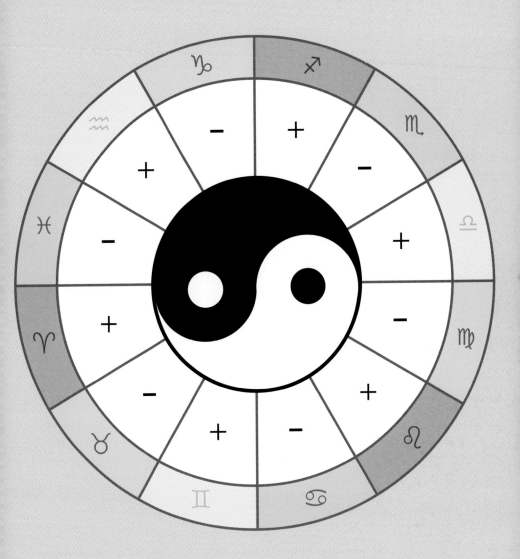

(Aries, Cancer, Libra, Capricorn) initiate new things; stable and change-resistant fixed signs (Taurus, Leo, Scorpio, Aquarius) prefer things to stay the same; flexible mutable signs (Gemini, Virgo, Sagittarius, Pisces) are happy to adapt and flow with life. When signs share the same quality, they want the same things from life and support each other in their efforts to attain them.

Active pairings

Aries–Libra

Aries is 'me'-oriented, Libra is partnership-oriented. With give and take on both sides, this is a stable and companionable pairing, provided Libra is not too laid-back or Aries overly demanding. Aries respects people who stand up for their rights but Libra avoids confrontation. In allowing Aries to take over, accommodating Libra can lose sight of personal needs.

LEARNING FROM ARIES Libra learns the value of confrontation. Straightforward Aries is attuned to the needs of 'me' and Libra is shown how to cut through indecision and learns how to recognize and fulfil its own inner needs without resorting to deviousness and manipulation. Aries never stays in a situation that is uncomfortable, nor does it suffer fools gladly. Aries simply states what it needs and expects those needs to be fulfilled.

LEARNING FROM LIBRA Aries learns about co-operation and weighing up the evidence before acting. Relationship-oriented Libra counterbalances the 'me first' attitude of Aries and develops partnerships based on 'what we need'. Adjustment is difficult for Aries, but Libra instinctively knows how to find compromise and harmony in a situation, and how to appreciate other people's points of view.

Gemini–Sagittarius

These signs complement each other on a journey of the mind. Unlikely to be a great physical passion, there are plenty of mental sparks and this pairing is productive intellectually. Sagittarius sees the bigger picture, but has the focus to pursue one thing deeply. Gemini gathers in disparate information, synthesizes it, and discusses it with the ever-willing-to-philosophize Sagittarius. The two rarely bore each other so the partnership lasts.

LEARNING FROM GEMINI Sagittarius can be carried away with enthusiasm. There is an insistence on talking about the latest obsession, be it project, person or idea. Sagittarius learns from Gemini a lightness of touch, discovering how to dance lightly over the surface of life. Subtlety and nuance are also found in Gemini.

LEARNING FROM SAGITTARIUS Sagittarius has a depth that fills the emptiness arising from lack of meaning that Gemini experiences. By attuning to Sagittarius, Gemini finds something to believe in. Sagittarius knows how to still the mind, to enter the contemplative space that allows Gemini to focus on the answers within.

Leo–Aquarius

Leo is a passionate, person-oriented sign and Aquarius is a dispassionate, people-centred sign but these two find much to admire in each other. Leo's benign warmth is attractive to Aquarius, and Aquarius' quirky eccentricity looks like fun to Leo. The more serious side of Aquarius appeals to warm-hearted Leo too, and provides an interesting challenge as Leo strives to entice Aquarius. Each sign values faithfulness and loyalty so the partnership is lasting and fulfilling.

LEARNING FROM LEO Aquarius is a cool sign but, by combining with Leo, Aquarius encounters heart-centred energy, uniting intimately with someone else. The personal self-awareness of Leo energizes and empowers detached Aquarian humanity, bringing forward-looking Aquarius into the spontaneity of the present moment.

LEARNING FROM AQUARIUS Aquarius takes a detached view of life which helps Leo to expand from a purely personal viewpoint to the wider scene. Aquarius values every human being and this overcomes a Leo tendency to look down on others. The unconventionality of Aquarius teaches Leo to loosen up, move away from a position of outraged dignity, and to have the courage to be different.

Passive pairings

Taurus–Scorpio

One of the most intense and magnetic pairings. Both have considerable staying power and match raw passion with sensuality, lust with controlled libido. While sex can become monotonous and mundane, the Taurus–Scorpio pairing has moments when torrid Scorpio takes them on a sexual high. Fixed signs value loyalty and continuity so the partnership lasts, and lasts. When all passion is spent, they stay together.

LEARNING FROM TAURUS The world of Scorpio is intense, dramatic and traumatic. From Taurus Scorpio learns how to grow steadily and life-enhancingly instead of death-defyingly. In Taurus Scorpio finds the inner security that makes the journey into the underworld safer and more certain of a fruitful return.

LEARNING FROM SCORPIO Fearless Scorpio has been down into the depths many times and survived. Confronting insecurities and darkness, Scorpio teaches Taurus to find inner security that cannot be shaken; and shows how to move beyond mortality into the prospect of immortality.

Cancer–Capricorn

These two are cardinal signs: each backs the other's ambition, both want success and work long and hard for it. The partnership is stable and lasting, and deeply sexual. The only problems arise when Capricorn, insists on getting to the top first; or when Cancer wants to put aside a lucrative career to care for a family. A Cancer man may be a house husband while his Capricorn spouse rules the boardroom. In the bedroom Capricorn is in control.

LEARNING FROM CANCER Cancer offers receptivity, nurturing and an emotional exchange that nourishes the Capricorn soul. Capricorn learns not to fear emotions and instinctual feelings. Discovering how to bend, to temper inner strength with compassion, to recognize the richness of feminine experience and to set aside masculine authoritarianism and a desire to control the world, Capricorn loosens up and enjoys life.

LEARNING FROM CAPRICORN Capricorn is much tougher than Cancer. A self-contained sign Capricorn does not allow emotion or sentiment to influence it. Cancer learns to resist the lure of emotional excess, to balance mood swings, and find safety. Capricorn's ability to let go and move on assists Cancer in dealing with a tendency to hold on to the past.

Virgo–Pisces

These two mutable signs are subtly attracted to each other. Virgo is hypnotized by Pisces' eyes, and uncharacteristically throws restraint to the wind when pursuing this slippery fish. However, the fact that Pisces is hard to pin down drives Virgo to distraction. Liking certainty in sex, not illusion, Virgo finds it hard to cope with Pisces' fantasies, especially those that take place in Pisces' head rather than in bed. Pisces admires Virgo's certainty and the efficiency with which this sign organizes life. A Virgo-Pisces pairing may stay together because the two need each other too much to part.

LEARNING FROM VIRGO Virgo's most valuable contribution to Pisces is the ability to discriminate, enabling Pisces to channel a compassionate nature into productive pursuits without risk of self-sacrifice. But Virgo also teaches Pisces the value of saying no – and meaning it. Virgo's clarity and directness in dealing with the day-to-day world is of enormous value to Pisces.

LEARNING FROM PISCES One of highly strung Virgo's problems can be compulsive behaviour and an inability to relax. Pisces teaches Virgo to go with the flow. Pisces' mystical connection to the greater whole assists Virgo to feel more accepted, releasing the need to criticize and control.

Venus and Mars

Venus and Mars are powerful significators of attraction. With strong pulling power, they create a love potion – or a poisoned chalice. If they connect across two charts, passion is unleashed; if they impact, they may well repel. They are at their most erotic in fire signs, their most persuasive in water signs, their most inventive in air signs and their most basic and lusty in earth signs.

Venus is a sociable planet and someone with a dominant Venus gives priority to relationships. A Venus-attuned person is amorous and attractive and not averse to using feminine wiles. In a man just as much as a woman, Venus may present as glamorous or prettily pleasing. This seductive planet puts out the message, blatantly or covertly, 'Come and get me, I'm yours' and imparts a voluptuousness that can be hard to resist, or a voraciousness that may repel. Venus can be surprisingly mercenary, adding an edge to a soft-hearted sun sign. But then Venus is not at all that she appears to be. Virile Mars is the conqueror, the original macho man who grabs what he wants, sweeping aside any opposition. The planet Mars is the symbol of lust and sexual drive, and zest for living, but Martian assertiveness can easily turn to aggression and cruelty. When Mars is strong desire will not be denied – even in a passive sun sign.

The placement of Venus and Mars in your birthchart shows the kind of sexual partners you are attracted to, describes your ideal lover, indicates your capacity for closeness and shows how you handle your intimate relations. The contacts that the passionate duo make across a pair of charts are potent. If the sun, Venus or Mars falls in the same sign in your chart as Venus, Mars or the sun in your partner's chart, magnetic attraction results. The attraction remains powerful but less immediate if the passionate pair fall in the same element (see page 110). If these planets are in incompatible elements or opposite polarities (see page 123), initial attraction can turn to repulsion. Mars in an active sign can be too aggressive and brash for a shy and retiring passive sign, which wants to be courted and wooed for hours, rather than moments. This turns Mars off, although misunderstandings and unnecessary force may ensue before pushy Mars gets the message. Where Venus is in an assertive active sign and Mars in the passive quality, Venus gets turned off first – much to the relief of Mars. There are times when Mars is strangely emasculated, when desire is leached away rather than stopped in its tracks. This usually occurs when Mars is in a receptive, watery sign but the air element can also have the effect of channelling all Mars's energy into fantasy rather than physical action.

Venus

Venus is desire that has taken on form. This glamorous planet is the idealized feminine and the darkest urges of your being. She is a predatory female, a voluptuary, or an untouchable sex goddess. The mythology of Venus is full of vanity and jealousy, rivalry and covetousness. The most treacherous and untamed of the goddesses, capricious Venus is rapacious lust, eroticism and devouring possessiveness. She is a passion that consumes you. Luscious and ripe, Venus is rampant sexual desire, however cunningly packaged. But Venus is also the sweet goddess of love and beauty. This is the pretty face and voluptuous figure that act like magnets to pleasure. Venus *is* the pleasure principle: a romantic image or a siren call. She shows how you answer the call of your desire nature.

Your sense of self and your own femininity are bound up in Venus. The goddess of love shows you how comfortable you are with yourself as a female and how you represent yourself to the outside world, the body language with which you express your sexuality, the kind of clothes you wear and how at home you are within your body. Depending upon the placement of Venus in your sign, Venus is glamorous, homely, sensuous, foxy, blatant, warm, frigid, manipulative or erotic. This planet is the mantle you wrap about you to indicate how you feel about yourself. Venus signifies how much value you place on yourself. It shows what you feel you deserve: happiness and pleasure or denial and repression. This planet describes your capacity to enjoy gratification of the senses and to indulge yourself. Venus is sensuality and the desire for power but also indicates your capacity for intimacy and closeness, or a flight into frigidity and fear. The planet represents your ideal woman and its placement in a man's chart shows the qualities you

seek in a partner, what you are attracted to and what turns you on. Venus reveals idealized qualities that are projected on to a woman who seems to be the ideal match. But if these qualities are not owned in yourself, the illusion turns sour, and the perfect woman becomes a virago who threatens to devour.

Seduction style

Venus in Aries	Blatant, there is no mistaking the ardour or intent.
Venus in Taurus	Slow and sensual, could anyone resist the promise of this much pleasure?
Venus in Gemini	You are talked out of your clothes and into bed without even noticing.
Venus in Cancer	The seductive crab sidles up, then the pincers catch hold.
Venus in Leo	This predatory lioness-in-heat mesmerizes her prey.
Venus in Virgo	The ambiance has to be exactly right before advances are made.
Venus in Libra	How can anyone resist when total attention is focused on them?
Venus in Scorpio	This sultry seductress comes on strong and never takes no for an answer.
Venus in Sagittarius	Bouncy, upfront and open but the impulse may not last.
Venus in Capricorn	Masterful planning lies behind carefully orchestrated advances.
Venus in Aquarius	Friendship comes first for this cool combination – seduction takes a while.
Venus in Pisces	You drown slowly in those melting eyes.

Venus around the zodiac

♈ Venus in Aries

This feisty combination is affectionate, selfish, self-centred and demanding – but irresistible! A sexual whirlwind, you act on impulse and follow desire. Venus in Aries can over-idealize partners who may not always appreciate your need for absolute honesty.

WHAT YOU SEEK A foxy lady: someone who is smart, independent and strong, who leads and who is not afraid to make her sexual needs known. The downside can be a selfish, bossy person.

♉ Venus in Taurus

This combination is sensual, lazy and acquisitive. Posing invitingly you turn on your sexual magnets and await results. Money and power attract you, as do beautiful things. Venus is at her most comfortable in hedonistic Taurus and you indulge yourself to the full. You need security in your relationship and tangible evidence of commitment before you succumb.

WHAT YOU SEEK A beautiful, faithful and voluptuous woman. Someone who cooks like a dream. Pragmatic home-making skills are as important as ripe sensuality. The flip side may be laziness.

♊ Venus in Gemini

This frothy combination makes you an engaging companion, but a capricious lover. Sociable and active, you thrive on variety, and love to flirt. Mental rapport is extremely important to you, much more so than physical compatibility or emotional connection.

WHAT YOU SEEK A charming, intelligent and quick-witted lover. An adaptable companion with whom discussion can take place is valued more than a wife. The reality may be a fickle, superficial shrew.

Venus in Cancer

This curvaceous combination is sentimental, clinging to the past. Moody and sensuous, you form exceedingly strong emotional attachments and are loathe to let these go. Nor are you keen to admit that your love may actually be founded on lust; you prefer the romantic ideal. What you crave is deep emotional sharing.

WHAT YOU SEEK A solicitous mother goddess who is cuddly and caressing. The flip side may be a crabby and sometimes hysterical, or a possessive, mother substitute.

Venus in Leo

This boisterous and playful combination gives off rampant sexual heat. Physically demonstrative, you want to adore your partner and be adored in return. Venus in Leo is glamorous and flamboyant, and can be vain. This is the sign of the poseur and yet you can also be exceedingly generous and kind-hearted.

WHAT YOU SEEK A sleek, magnificent and oh so slightly dangerous lioness; the kind who is well fed and playful after the kill. The reality may be a snarling virago or a drama queen.

Venus in Virgo

This repressive combination can be coolly critical and somewhat frigid until roused, when your earthy sensuality comes to the fore. But you keep your emotions firmly in check; being carried away is not for you. You need a partner who is on the same mental wavelength and who can appreciate your cool ardour.

WHAT YOU SEEK A perfect woman, with refined sensuality and an excellent mind. The downside can be a lover who is prissy, prudish and nit-picking.

♎ Venus in Libra

This erotically pleasing combination was made for love. You feel complete when in a relationship, and may well mask your true feelings in order to be liked or to keep the peace. You seek harmony above all things and choose to believe that you are romantically in love when what you want is sensual, sybaritic gratification.

WHAT YOU SEEK A vision of charming perfection. Accommodating and pleasing, this lover shows little outward sign of the selfish virago who lurks beneath the surface.

♏ Venus in Scorpio

This smouldering combination is charismatic and seductive but lethal jealousy lurks in your heart. To you love is an intense affair: this is the side of Venus that would kill to get what she wants. Your affairs are often conducted in secret and you rarely share all your thoughts or feelings with a partner.

WHAT YOU SEEK A femme fatale, a mystery woman with sexual charisma who intrigues. The flip side is that she is highly manipulative with a sting in the tail.

♐ Venus in Sagittarius

This flighty combination finds commitment exceedingly difficult; you want to take your pleasure where you will. Passionate and easily roused you may be, but intense you are not, and you often have sexual adventures just for fun.

WHAT YOU SEEK An intellectual courtesan: a charming companion who makes few demands but who is always willing to entertain. The flip side is a lover who shows a lack of commitment and is easily bored.

♑ Venus in Capricorn

This steely combination cools Venus' ardour. You are undemonstrative and cautious. To the outside world you appear cold. Looking for stability in relationships, you have no difficulty in controlling your strong libido and delaying consummation. The difficulty lies in showing affection and in actually feeling your feelings, which you tend to repress as you block emotional expression.

WHAT YOU SEEK A powerful, successful woman. The downside may be a lover who is bossy, authoritarian and cold.

♒ Venus in Aquarius

This dispassionate combination finds deep emotions difficult to handle. You prefer friendship. It is not that you do not have passionate emotions, you do, but your rational mind stands back from them in bewilderment and you have sincere difficulty with emotional expression. Your sexual proclivities may be kinky and a bit unusual.

WHAT YOU SEEK Whatever your ideal it is *different* and possibly bizarre. You need a wacky woman but may find you have attracted someone who is totally off the wall.

♓ Venus in Pisces

This gullible combination sacrifices all for love and the romantic dream. Soft-hearted, vulnerable and in love with the idea of being in love, you drift from one relationship to another without actually ending any. As a result you find yourself a victim of love and cannot distinguish between love and lust. When you do fall in love, you want mystical union.

WHAT YOU SEEK A beautiful dream made flesh; but the problem lies in distinguishing what is real from what is illusion. Confusion abounds.

Mars

Mars is lust that has taken on form. This virile planet is sexual desire and passion, masculinity and aggression, ardour and potency. It is a primitive, competitive, initiatory force born out of the drive towards procreation and conquest. Frequently crude and insensitive, Mars describes how courtship and sex are approached; how assertive you are in pursuing your objective; and how well your libido flows.

Mars is related to intense human experiences: power, anger and passion. How you handle these affects all your relationships. If you are self-assured and effective, you feel good, and attract beneficial relationships. To be in control of your power, and to be self-assertive, Mars must function well. However, when Mars does not, you feel helpless and out of control, and attract destructive relationships and feel vulnerable to passion. Passion is the intensity with which you can abandon yourself in the moment. The placement of Mars in your chart shows how much you are able to express your passion. Frigidity and impotence arise from denial of passion.

Mars can be an antisocial planet because it is wrapped up in personal needs. It manifests as assertion or aggression, anger or angst, apathy or rage. When Mars is particularly strong, cruelty and control may be a problem, power trips become the norm and violence lies just beneath the surface. When Mars is weak manipulation, appeasement, sacrifice and neediness come into play. The person fears that in standing up for his or her personal needs, others are displeased. Conversely control is often exerted through threat of loss of love. There can be problems with passive aggression, and great difficulty in saying no. But by always saying yes, Mars has nothing to bounce off. Healthy relationships need the frisson of disagreements and differing viewpoints.

Mars also represents will and the element in which Mars is placed affects how your will manifests. Mars in fire is strong-willed and assertive; but with Mars in water you have difficulty expressing your will no matter how strong this is. With Mars in air you have no difficulty in expressing what you want, but stamina and willpower are lacking; while Mars in earth is strong-willed and yet may suffer from inertia. However, once you set your will towards something, nothing dissuades you.

In a woman's chart Mars describes the type of man to whom you are attracted, showing the qualities of your ideal man. The planet shows how much of your own assertive or aggressive energies you live out for yourself and how much is lived out by a partner.

Elemental passion

Mars in fire	Passion tends to be volcanic, bursting out spontaneously, sweeping all before it. There is little build-up, and hardly any control.
Mars in earth	There is a pragmatic approach to passion, which can be controlled, but libido is strong and passion can run high.
Mars in air	Passion is mental rather than physical and a great idea is more of a turn-on than a pretty face. Libido can be put aside in favour of more pressing concerns.
Mars in water	Passion lies beneath the surface and is often repressed. Romantic water signs savour the feelings of each moment: you live in the passion of your emotions.

Mars around the zodiac

♈ Mars in Aries

With this bold placement you see what you want and go all out for it. Raunchy Mars in Aries is selfish, competitive, and rarely takes no for an answer. Desire burns brightly, libido is strong and immediate satisfaction is demanded – although this pushy combination lacks stamina and may not stay the course.

WHAT YOU SEEK An energetic, independent, brash and adventurous man; although the machismo, over-competitiveness and temper that accompanies Mars in Aries may prove less than ideal.

♉ Mars in Taurus

With this enduring placement you have a strong, earthy sensuality, and a powerful control over your body. Desire may be reined in so sexual release is all the greater when it occurs, but randy Taurus has no hang-ups about sexual expression.

WHAT YOU SEEK A solid, stable and reliable man with wealth and status. This determined placement reflects a strong sex drive and commitment to home and family, but can have a spectacular temper when aroused.

♊ Mars in Gemini

This talkative placement is the signal for friendly persuasion and open-minded sex. With Mars in Gemini you talk yourself into bed, bedazzling the object of your infatuation. Gemini passion is fuelled by words, and much of it happens in your head despite Mars' predisposition to short-term action.

WHAT YOU SEEK A slim, wiry, intelligent, witty and entertaining man. The versatility and multi-facetedness of Gemini appeals, although a devious nature can cause problems.

♋ Mars in Cancer

With this tenacious placement you are cautious about expressing passion, even when it runs high. Cancer approaches circuitously, succumbing to Mars' urges at the last moment, but the sex drive can fluctuate wildly. Once ignited there is no stopping you. You show your passion through caring for your beloved.

WHAT YOU SEEK A protective, caring, concerned, sensitive and emotional lover. A tendency to bury anger, which can lead to hidden aggression and constant irritation.

♌ Mars in Leo

With this combustible placement you are proud with a strong libido and can burn with passion, but tend to wait to attract rather than pursing the object of your desire. Mars in dramatic Leo is sometimes over-powering and larger than life, and your bawdy fantasies are acted out with great enthusiasm.

WHAT YOU SEEK This courtly combination idolizes powerful men who may be confident to the point of arrogance. However, the desire is for a benevolent dictator rather than the autocrat who may lurk beneath the benign exterior.

♍ Mars in Virgo

With this prudish placement you are somewhat prissy about expressing passion freely, until nature takes over and your earthy sexuality comes into play. Mars in Virgo strives to overcome a tendency towards sexual hang-ups and modesty, but your sex drive remains firmly controlled and you consider things carefully before acting. Your willpower is passive and restrained and your fear of making a mistake holds you back from expressing your natural urges.

WHAT YOU SEEK An intelligent, witty and painstaking man. A perfectionist who has high standards and who may criticize if ideals are not met.

♎ Mars in Libra

With this pleasure-loving placement you are charming but weak-willed and easily seduced. In laid-back Libra Mars finds great difficulty in saying no, and you may well find yourself accommodating someone else's passion. Although, if roused sufficiently, you force your own desires on others.

WHAT YOU SEEK A physically beautiful, well-mannered and courteous lover; charm is all important, and knowing how to please a partner. The downside can be a vain and lazy charmer who prefers to live off women or who takes a passive role in relationship.

♏ Mars in Scorpio

This highly sexed placement is the most powerful in the zodiac, giving you a magnetic aura of power. When thwarted, ruthless Mars in Scorpio can be exceedingly cruel and jealousy is a problem, as are psychological power trips.

WHAT YOU SEEK Enigmatic, intense and magnetic; you seek a mystery man who is 'bad, mad and dangerous to know'. Loyalty and fidelity are valued but the adrenaline charge of a bad relationship is seductive for this destructive combination, and power games are common.

♐ Mars in Sagittarius

Enthusiastic and passionate. With Mars in philosophical Sagittarius your passion may be for something other than libidinous urges. Quests beckon you onwards. Once Mars gets down to it, the sex is adventurous, but this is an uncommitted placement of the planet.

WHAT YOU SEEK A devil-may-care, freedom-loving adventurer who roams far and wide in search of answers. While philosophical discussion is a turn-on, Sagittarius' lack of commitment and inevitable tendency to tactlessness is not.

♑ Mars in Capricorn

This placement is exceedingly horny. With lusty Mars in ruthless Capricorn you throw caution to the wind when the rutting season gets underway. Uncharacteristically for this controlled sign, libido can lead you astray. Capricorn's staying power is appreciated by your partner.

WHAT YOU SEEK A masterful, authoritative and successful man; power turns on Mars in Capricorn. He may be older or a father-figure. The downside is a cold, authoritarian and steely control freak, who puts feelings aside in favour of success and who demands absolute obedience.

♒ Mars in Aquarius

This deviant placement is not a happy combination. Dispassionate and detached, Aquarius holds back lusty Mars with cool caution. Living in your head, you prefer airy fantasy, an internet chat room or experimental sex to unrestrained physical passion. Voyeuristic at heart, fearing intimacy, you may opt for celibacy.

WHAT YOU SEEK A dispassionate, coolly sexual and controlled lover, 'quirky and interesting' with something *different* to offer and yet rebellious of heart. Mars in Aquarius is an androgynous figure, curiously devoid of potency.

♓ Mars in Pisces

With this vulnerable placement you confuse lust with love and need with passion, and your bleeding heart is taken advantage of. Your sex drive fluctuates and is strongly affected by mood. Impressionable Mars in Pisces would rather be pursued by than pursue the object of desire, and libido can lose its way; but you have the power to hypnotize your victim into bed.

WHAT YOU SEEK A dream lover made flesh. He is suave, romantic and charming, but slippery like a fish and impossible to pin down.

Index

Acknowledgements

Executive Editor Brenda Rosen
Managing Editor Clare Churly
Executive Art Editor Sally Bond
Designer Martin Lovelock
Illustrator Andrew Pavitt
Production Controller Aileen O'Reilly